FLIPPING
MAIN STREET

How to Flip Houses Without Going Upside Down

JERRY AGEE & TERENCE DAVIS

Published by Best Seller Publishing®, St. Augustine, FL
Best Seller Publishing® is a registered trademark
Printed in the United States of America.
ISBN: 978-1-956649-49-9

This publication is designed to provide accurate and authoritative information with regard to the subject matter covered. It is sold with the understanding that the publisher is not engaged in rendering legal, accounting, or other professional advice. If legal advice or other expert assistance is required, the services of a competent professional should be sought. The opinions expressed by the authors in this book are not endorsed by Best Seller Publishing® and are the sole responsibility of the author rendering the opinion.

Most Best Seller Publishing® titles are available at special quantity discounts for bulk purchases for sales promotions, premiums, fundraising, and educational use. Special versions or book excerpts can also be created to fit specific needs.

For more information, please write:
Best Seller Publishing®
53 Marine Street
St. Augustine, FL 32084
or call 1(626) 765 9750
Toll Free: 1(844) 850-3500
Visit us online at: www.BestSellerPublishing.org

FOREWARD

Wisdom. This one word describes this book. I personally have purchased 100s of millions of dollars of real estate. Having had the wisdom of this book and applied it would have saved me years of time and millions of dollars.

Would you prefer to earn a hundred dollars an hour or the same amount every minute? It is the same amount of money; what is different is the cycle-time. The knowledge in this book dramatically reduces cycle-time. This means absorbing and implementing its wisdom will greatly accelerate your financial wealth.

Experience is a great teacher. Yet it is not the best way to learn. If experience was the best teacher then America would have a stranglehold on making the best cars. Clearly that is not the case. Other areas of the world make excellent vehicles despite having less experience.

How did this happen? The other countries learned fast. They acquired and implemented different theories, methods and tools on how to build excellent vehicles. This knowledge propelled their success.

Almost everyone who becomes super successful studied with at least one master. It was the master who provided many of the insights that created success.

The same is true for buying and selling real estate. This book is written by two masters of real estate. The authors share how to make millions in this field by discovering and adding value to real property. The underlying component is a basic system of acquiring real estate below market value, adding value through renovation, and reselling it for profit. By adding website support they have deepened their predictable success method.

This book offers you much more than a "how-to" real estate investing book. It provides an opportunity for personal interaction with true masters. All you have to do to fully engage these masters is visit www.flippingmainstreet.com. The Accountability Program offered there is just one way to interact.

Wealth or lack, are framed by one's beliefs. It is an intrinsic process that comes first and the extrinsic results (the financial wealth) follows. The good news is that you can change your beliefs.

Follow the Flipping Main Street process. When you do, many will experience a "belief system" change. The theories, methods and tactics espoused in this book create the environment for this to happen.

This is a dynamic process. Relax and enjoy the experience.

Marshall Thurber
Real Estate Investor, Attorney and Perpetual Student.

TABLE OF CONTENTS

Thank you to these extraordinary people who continue challenging us to be examples and not warnings…

Willa
Alden
Daschiel
Archer
Ava Jude

CHAPTER 1

WHY

Why real estate, why us, and why this book? Most books about real estate investing primarily focus on the money, but our approach is more holistic. Our book is written from a win-win viewpoint, solving problems for distressed sellers and making money for our partners and investors, while creating jobs and income for our contractor partners, better homes for our community, and better lives for ourselves. This book tells you in simple terms how to create a system to harness the best outcome possible and build a business from scratch. It will also help you avoid many of the failures that slow or stop investors from finding long-term success in real estate.

It starts with you. It starts with the reason or reasons you chose this book. You didn't choose the latest romance or mystery novel; you chose a book with a title that suggests making a radical change in your life through real estate. So our first questions to you are: Why? Why are you trying to make a change? What is motivating you?

It's usually a combination of factors, but it might be that you want to work for yourself and have more freedom in your schedule and life in general. Maybe you want more flexibility to be at your kids' school performances or field trips, or perhaps you want more time to volunteer in your community, be with friends and family, or work on yourself. Maybe you have a terrible boss or co-workers, and you dread going to work every day. Or maybe you're getting older, and you are struggling with a physically demanding job that you worry you won't be able to do for much longer. Maybe you feel stifled by your current job, and you yearn to do something more creative. Or, of course, it could be about the money. Maybe you have juggled bills for so long that it has become your normal. Maybe you realize your kids are just a few years away from college, and you have nothing saved. Maybe you're thinking, forget the kids, I'm only a few years from retirement, and I don't have anything saved for myself!

The good news is that the plan we have laid out in this book can solve your financial problems. But while the extra money might make life a little easier, it doesn't always make it happier. So try to start this project with a clear picture of your other *whys*. Even if you're doing this because you want more money to take a big family trip or pay for your daughter's wedding, realize that it's not about the money. Even in these examples, the *why* is that you want to spend more time with or take care of the people you love. That is a far bigger *why* than simply thinking, "I need $10,000 by next summer." When your *why* is clear, your motivation will be much more powerful.

You might be wondering what our *whys* were when we first started investing in real estate. We think you will see that they probably weren't much different than yours are now.

Terence's Why

In the spring of 2001, I had a lot going on. I was in the process of moving back to my hometown of Redding, California, opening a real estate office, and planning my wedding. My fiancé was still finishing her school year as a teacher in Sacramento, so I was going back and forth between Redding and Sacramento each week so we could work on wedding planning.

While it might have made more sense simply to rent an apartment in Redding while we made the transition, I was determined to own our first home before we were married. And unfortunately for us, I was dead set on finding the best deal possible. Even though I was selling new homes in a development for $150,000 at the time, we were still paying off tens of thousands of dollars in student loans, and I wanted to find something well under $100,000 so the payment would be low enough to keep the property as a future rental.

Even then, I was envisioning building my real estate portfolio. I had worked as an agent in both commercial and residential real estate, first in Los Angeles, then in Sacramento, and now back in Redding. My first two jobs in real estate were with investment real estate companies, and that training gave me a great foundation for understanding value.

Most of the houses we found in the five-digit range were junk or in bad neighborhoods, but we finally found a HUD foreclosure on a quiet, tree-lined street, just two blocks from the middle school we had both attended as kids. It was a three bedroom, one bath with dead grass and cockroaches, and it had been home to a family of cats for months, maybe years, while it sat vacant.

The opening bid on the property was $70,000, but we knew there would be competition, so we offered $84,000. We kicked ourselves later when we learned the next highest bid was $80,000, but we were so excited to own our first home that it didn't matter, even though the extra $4,000 was more than we were spending on our wedding, now just a month away.

There was no air-conditioning in the house, and June in Redding can bring 100-degree temperatures, so we almost called off the wedding one sweltering night as we battled with a commercial floor sander and each other, and nearly succumbed to the noise, sawdust, and sweat. When it was over 90 degrees, the swamp cooler blasted out nothing but warm, damp air. Still, we would stand under it every night, hoping for one gasp of anything cold.

We pulled carpet staples from the hardwood floors, scrubbed filth, and swept up cat hair for days on end. We painted and did all the cheap, dumb labor we could while our prized $10-an-hour handyman set tile and rebuilt the rotten kitchen floor. We got help from every family member who would show up for free lunch. Neighbors came to visit and told us stories about the old attorney who had died in the sunken family room and the family who had lived there in the 1960s and kept a pet monkey in a cage on the porch. There were many days when we regretted not buying the new house in a subdivision that didn't have any weird stories or troubling history.

We made it through the wedding on a miraculously cool July day, which was an incredible blessing if you know Redding in the summertime. We had a one-night honeymoon in a bed and breakfast two miles from our house and got back to work the next day.

The miserably hot days turned cold really fast in October, and we still had nothing but two space heaters that we had borrowed from family. Those heaters followed us around like R2-D2 while we walked around the house in knit caps and layers of sweatshirts. Our handyman cleaned the chimney, and I'll always remember how excited my wife was when she came home from work on a freezing October night and found a fire burning in the fireplace. It was a great moment. An even better moment was when we put in central heat and air-conditioning that November.

We continued to work on that little house in fits and starts over the next few years, and eventually, we refinanced it to get a down payment on a beautiful new home in our favorite neighborhood. In the spring of 2005, we sold our little Gold Street house for $238,000—just over triple what we had paid for it four years earlier.

Would it have been easier to rent a nice apartment with heat and air-conditioning? Couldn't we have taken more weekend trips if we weren't working on that house all the time? Maybe, but the equity from that simple little house allowed us to invest in several other investment properties, some of which I'll discuss later. It also helped us to start another real estate business and buy an office building, that I still own and I hope will be a big part of my retirement one day. All of this came from making the decision to buy a run-down little house for $84,000.

My *why* was that I wanted more than anything to build a strong future for my family. I had grown up with divorce and a fair amount of instability. My primary *why* was very simple: I wanted a better life for my children. And after spending my entire 20s struggling with school loans, I wanted freedom from worrying about debt and stressing over bills, and the simple luxury of a little bit of down time to dream and be creative. I knew I wasn't going to get these things by living in an apartment or continuing to run up credit cards or other debt.

So if you don't own a home, or if you have school loans and debt, should you run out and buy the first junky house that seems like a good opportunity and enjoy life while you wait for it to triple? If you said yes, you weren't paying attention to the story. Remember, we shopped—and shopped. I studied the market and looked at every house in our price range, and we bought the worst house in the best area. You can always change a house, but you can't change a neighborhood, and you can't move railroad tracks, a freeway, or a floodplain. Did we just hope that it was going to be a good opportunity and that the market would go up? No. We studied the market and knew we were still at the bottom of the market. We had a pretty good idea about where we were in the cycle. The Bay Area and Sacramento markets were already surging, but the prices in Redding had been stagnant for six or seven years. While we were shopping for our house, one long-time local informed me, "No house in the Garden Tract will ever be worth more than $100,000." I'm glad I didn't listen to him! We also didn't just sit back and wait for the market. We put in the work—blood, sweat, tears, and even an electrical shock from a loose wire touching an iron pipe during one day of rehab. We were both working full-time jobs, my wife as a new teacher and I as a real estate agent in a new market, and we still made time to sand floors, prime, paint, and scrub. And scrub. And scrub.

Did we live like real estate moguls and take lavish trips with our six-figure equity? No, while we worked on the house, we put aside every penny we could to pay off our college loans and credit card debt. In four years of sacrifice, by the time we purchased our second home, we had paid our nearly six-figure debt in full. At that time, it seemed like everyone was buying new cars, boats, and fancy toys, yet we kept driving our 10-year-old Hondas. We kept our foundation strong by getting rid of debt and keeping our expenses low.

The long-term goal is to grow income and reduce, freeze, or minimize spending. This is how you will grow assets and build wealth. Surprising as it may sound, lasting wealth is typically not built by people with large incomes, but by those with steady savings and conservative assets that grow over time.

I have seen hundreds of real estate agents, investors, and contractors who are consistently at the top of their field, yet also consistently spend more than they make. As soon as there is any correction in the market or they run into one bad investment, their entire paper empire comes crashing down. Had they just controlled their debt and spending, they wouldn't have had to keep starting over. I have a broker/developer colleague who has done this three times in his life. He is now in his 70s and has just climbed back out of the debt he accrued during the last market downturn. He did just buy a third vacation home and has some other expensive hobbies, so my guess is that as soon as the market hits the next slowdown, he will crash with it all over again.

A final note on saving versus spending, especially as it pertains to real estate professionals: The typical and very dangerous cycle that affects real estate professionals, including agents, lenders, contractors, and investors, is that because they are the earliest and worst hit when the market takes a downturn, they often face a complete financial meltdown that can lead to bankruptcy, foreclosures, divorce, and depression. As a result, when market prices reach their lowest and most attractive entry point, these people have bad credit, crushed egos, no capital, and no ability to participate in the best market for finding opportunities. As the market starts to improve again, these same professionals slowly start to recover, pay off debt, improve their credit, and accumulate savings, and they typically start buying in at the very peak of the market cycle. The very people who should know better end up being the last ones to enter the market before it crashes—and they end up riding the rollercoaster right down to the bottom again.

Meanwhile, the smart investors are carefully saving their acorns, driving their boring cars, and cooking at home instead of going out for sushi four nights a week. They snicker when some novice agent tells them about a "deal" at the top of the market cycle that has negative cash flow or has already tripled in value over the last five years. They are waiting, hoarding their capital, and when the market is reduced to a smoking ruin, they grab up all those little Monopoly houses for 40 cents on the dollar and add them to their long-term income and retirement plan. These are the people truly building wealth. This is the path we wish for you. And if you do it right, you can still have sushi every once in a while.

Jerry's Why

For the last six years, I have lived in Nosara, Costa Rica. It's a tropical paradise that looks like a postcard come to life with monkeys in the trees, flowers, fruit trees, and a five-mile white sand beach with an incredible surf break that I paddle out in most mornings. It also happens to be the yoga capital of Central America, and that is not bad if you don't mind looking at beautiful, healthy people from all over the world. Before that, I lived in Park City, Utah, where I had a beautiful 8,500-square-foot home with an indoor pool. Park City has the best snow on earth. I learned to love the outdoors again by snowboarding and hiking and biking. And before living in Utah, I lived in Hollywood, California, and worked in the entertainment industry as a producer. I was traveling in Russell, New Zealand, with my amazing wife Khel on our second wedding anniversary when I realized I was essentially retired at 32 years old. Sounds like a pretty amazing life, right?

Well, it is, and it all came from investing in real estate and from a simple question I had asked myself less than two years before retiring. That question, you guessed it, was: Why? Though it may seem trivial, it is important because it gives clarity, and clarity is power. For that reason, it's worth writing down your *why* and having it around you. The clearer you are about your *why*, the more precise you can be with your plan.

The word *plan* makes many people's stomachs tighten. Nevertheless, you must have one. Whether you follow that plan to make a little extra cash, go on a nice trip or buy a new car or something mundane like hardwood floors in your home, you must have a plan. I have met with coaching clients who have told me they want to make more money, so I would just reach in my pocket and give them five bucks and say, "All right, now you have more money; now what?"

My *why* was to spend more time with the woman I loved. More than anything in the world, that was my *why*. My wife was my better half by far, as I'm sure Terence would agree. It all meant nothing if I didn't get to share time with her. When I was working crazy 14-hour days in the entertainment industry, I asked myself *why* when it didn't create anything of importance but was more of a distraction. Then it came to me that I just wanted to spend more time with Khel. I wanted to travel and have fun with her. I wanted to do the things we loved together. And I wanted to play and work with friends. It was imperative to me to find a way to have time with my lady and my friends, not be stressed out about money, and be able to create something. That was my *why* over 15 years ago.

If you ask me today, my *why* has changed. Khel passed away from cancer in 2010 but graced me with our beautiful son, who was born the year before she died. I also have a daughter now, and my biggest *why* today is to be an example for my children rather than a warning. I want to show my children what I care about. I care about them and what they are doing, and I want them to care about each other and other people in the world. Spending time with them is paramount to me. If I had a grinding job that kept me away from them, they wouldn't get to see who I am and how I handle both the big and little things life throws our way. I want to show them my belief system, but ultimately give them the creativity, strength, and freedom to choose their own system of beliefs. It's a core value of mine to pass that kind of freedom to my children.

When you identify your *why*, and it aligns with your core values and beliefs, you become unstoppable.

I didn't start out on the right side of the tracks. There were no silver spoons in my house. I was brought up in the lower class. I was the youngest of five siblings, and we had a mom who loved and cared for us. We were never taught about money but were taught to love each other and be good to one another. It wasn't until I was out on my own that I learned about finance.

Though I became a self-made millionaire by the age of 32, I had not sought to become wealthy but to become a better person—another big *why* throughout my life. I wanted to become a person my wife could be proud of, my friends would look up to, and my children could learn from, and I'm proud of who I am today. I have been there for my twelve-year-old his entire life, making sure that he has seen more of the world by twelve than most people see in two lifetimes, creating a secure and stable home for him, and giving him a life in a tropical paradise, but still nurturing his connection to my family and his mom's family, even when that means racking up tens of thousands of miles each year on our frequent flier cards. He now has a little sister, and I am working to ensure the same access to life, learning, and family for her.

I have built more castles and dug more holes on the beach than anyone could ever imagine, and I have gotten to play with Legos and boats, make up fantastic games and stories, and attend nearly every single school function. I was there for my friends when they got married—everybody but Terence, oddly enough. That is what's important in life. It's not to have numbers with a lot of zeroes in your bank account. It's to live life.

Continue asking yourself, why? It will give you great clarity and enable you to draw your plan, which we will go into in coming chapters. Be clear about what you want and what your goals are. Then you will be able to handle all the not-so-ideal situations that are going to come up along the way.

The reason I'm able to have this clarity is that I did ask myself *why* and continue to do so every year or less. I can have the lifestyle I have now and live in two countries and travel the world with my kids all because of real estate.

It's easy; it's not simple, but it is easy. You just have to ask yourself: What is my *why*? To make it a little easier, we have included a worksheet on the next page so that you can get clear on your *why*.

Turn the page and get started. Fill it out as completely and honestly as you can. Spend 15 minutes (we all have 15 minutes for our future!) to make your future that much clearer and that much better. Then we will jump into the next chapter, which will be the nuts and bolts of how to make your first million in real estate.

WORKSHEET: WHY

It's very easy in this digital and media-heavy age to grade ourselves against Forbes billionaires, rock stars, start-up geniuses, and super-human athletes making eight-figure incomes, but it can very easily set us up for failure before we even start.

Try instead to grade yourself against your own *why* and nothing else. Don't compare yourself to your friends that took over a thriving family business, or the neighbors who inherited 50 million bucks. When you focus on what brings you happiness and stop worrying about everything and everybody else, your job becomes a whole lot easier without a lot of negative self-talk or self-judgment. If your goal is to become the next real estate billionaire, and if that is the only thing that will bring you fulfillment and happiness, then we are behind you all the way. Just make sure there is a *why* in there that isn't only about the money. If you need some inspiration, visit our website: www.flippingmainstreet.com.

You might already be familiar with the following story; Whether you have heard it before or not, please take the time to read it and do the five-minute exercise that follows.

It was a warm spring day at the college. The birds were singing, the grass on campus had turned green, and the air was filled with the sweet scent of apple blossom.

The lecture hall was full that day. The dull roar of about 100 students talking and bantering filled the room before the bell rang and the professor walked in. The professor was a tall, slender man with soft white hair and a beard like Santa Claus. He wore khaki shorts, flip-flops, and a flaming red button-down Hawaiian shirt.

When the class began, he wordlessly picked up a large, empty jar and proceeded to fill it with golf balls. He then asked the students, "Is the jar full?" They agreed that it was.

The professor said, "No, it's not."

The class sat in silence.

He then picked up a box of pebbles and poured them into the jar. He shook the jar lightly. The pebbles rolled into the open areas between the golf balls. He then asked the students again if the jar was full. Again, they said it was.

"No, it's not."

Again, there was silence from the audience.

The professor next picked up a box of sand and poured it into the jar. The sand filled up everything else. He asked once more if the jar was full. The students responded with a unanimous "yes!"

"No, it's not."

The professor then produced two beers from under the table and poured the entire contents into the jar effectively filling the empty space between the sand. The students laughed.

"Now," said the professor as the laughter subsided, "I want you to recognize that this jar represents your life. The golf balls are the important things—your family, your friends, your health, your favorite endeavors—and if everything else was lost and only the golf balls remained, your life would still be full. The pebbles are the other things that matter like your job, your house, and your car. The sand is everything else—the small stuff."

"If you put the sand into the jar first," he continued, "there is no room for the pebbles or the golf balls. The same goes for life. If you spend all your time and energy on the small stuff, you will never have room for the things that are important to you."

One of the students raised her hand and inquired what the beer represented. The professor smiled warmly and said, "I'm glad you asked." "The beer just shows you that no matter how full your life may seem, there's always room for a couple of beers with a friend."

The professor then lowered his glasses on his nose, raised one brow, and said, "How many of you are filling your jar with sand instead of golf balls today?"

EXERCISE

Step 1

Write down the answers next to the questions.

1. What are your golf balls?

2. What are your pebbles?

3. What is your sand?

Don't read ahead until you have finished Step 1. This is very, very, very important. Are you done?

Now move on to Step 2.

Step 2

As above, *write down* the answers next to the questions. Don't move on to the last step, Step 3, until you are finished.

1. Tell me what your life would look like in three years if you only had sand in your jar?

    Would you have the things you want in your life?

    How does that make you feel?

2. Tell me what your life would look like in three years if you had only pebbles in your jar?

    Would you have reached your goals?

    How does that make you feel?

3. Tell me what your life would look like in three years if you had only golf balls in your jar?

    Would you be more of what you wanted to be?

    How does that make you feel?

    Have you done Step 2 in full? Move on to Step 3.

Step 3 (If you have time and you should make time.)

Go back to Step 2 and read each question and your answer.

1. How does your body feel and how do you feel when you read question 1 and your answer? *Write this down.*

2. How does your body feel and how do you feel when you read question 2 and your answer? *Write this down.*

3. How does your body feel and how do you feel when you read question 3 and your answer? *Write this down.*

Through this exercise, you should have found your *why*. When you read that *why*, you feel an empty pit in your stomach or well up with pride or tears. So write down that *why*, keep it close to you in your purse or your wallet, and look at it every day for 10 days. Envision yourself being the person who owns their *why* and is an example to people around them about what a full life looks like.

Now have an amazing day!

CHAPTER 2

BECOME A STUDENT

The first thing you need to do is go out and look at 100 houses. You will learn a lot by walking through that number of houses. Among other things, you will learn what styles are selling, what styles are not, what styles are too edgy, and what things are just functionally obsolete. For example, in most rural and suburban markets today, carports are not very sought after. People want two-car or three-car garages. Everyone has a lot more stuff than they did 50 years ago when carports were in vogue. In 10 years, we will probably see buyers in the suburbs and rural areas expecting four-car garages!

You can learn about some of these trends by picking up magazines and watching Sunday afternoon TV, but to get a thorough knowledge of what works and what doesn't, you need to study your local market. Make it a point to do so before you start investing. Buyers today like granite, marble, or quartz countertops, and sometimes even expect granite or marble countertops, great subway tile, custom paint, hardwood floors, and dramatic lighting with Edison bulbs. So when every finish in a house pre-dates 1970, you will know that there will be some work to do.

Study the Market

Terence

I have rarely bought new cars, but three years ago I bought a brand-new car with all the upgrades and options. My commute from my home to my office is only three miles, and there are many days I end up doing most of my work from home. But somehow, I have 96,000 miles on my barely three-year-old vehicle.

So how did this happen? It happened because every time I see a potential opportunity, I just get in the car and check it out. When competitors put a new project on the market, or when one of my contractors tells me about a renovation they are working on, I try to take a look at those as well. I could probably disqualify two-thirds of these properties from my desk, but I have always found that I learn more by getting out and seeing things firsthand. By doing this over and over again, I know not only every neighborhood, but which cul-de-sac has bad neighbors or ugly power lines or even which specific houses were built by the worst developers back in the 1970s.

Contractors can tell you all about their best work, but you must go and look at their current projects to see how they run a job. Getting out and studying these projects also gives you the chance to meet subcontractors, agents, and neighbors. If you get to know the contractors or vendors who are handling the trash-outs or yard maintenance for the bank-owned homes in your area, they will probably be able to tell you about other opportunities—the ones that just need carpet and paint, or the great one that is coming on the market next week.

Terence

I was recently getting bids on stucco and felt like they were all coming in too high. I knew there was a subdivision of new homes being built, so I drove out and found a stucco crew hard at work on one of the homes. I sat in my car and made calls while I watched their progress to see how much work a five-man crew could get done in an hour. It confirmed for me that the stucco bid I had just gotten was about $3,000 too high, and I was able to get a lower price because I knew what the contractor's costs were. If you're going to put your time, money, and effort into becoming a real estate investor, you must study every aspect of the real estate market.

Observe Trustee Sales

If this seems overwhelming, just start by looking in your local newspaper's classified section and find the trustee sale section. It will tell you the location and time of the trustee sales. Go tomorrow and simply watch. Remember, you are a student. When you learn to drive, you don't just jump into the driver's seat and hope you will learn by doing! Watching the trustee sales doesn't require finding an agent or even making a phone call or finding a project to drive by. You don't even have to talk to anyone when you get there if you don't want to; all you have to do is watch and listen.

Some of the investors there might start a conversation with you to find out who you are and what you're doing there. When you tell them you are a new real estate investor, half of them will ignore you and not want to share information, and the other half will probably start telling you more than you ever wanted to know—most likely a lot of horror stories to scare you away. The nicer ones might tell you the address of a house they are currently working on that you can go look at. If all you do is show up two or three days per week for one hour at a time, you will pick up more valuable information from talking with these people than you could gain from a four-year degree in real estate.

Most trustee sales are scheduled for a specific time, but more often than not, they get delayed for 30 minutes at a time while last-minute paperwork gets reviewed, or trustees make sure they have handled the foreclosure properly. An 11:00 a.m. sale can easily get delayed to 11:30, then again to noon, then to 12:30, and finally postponed for a week or month at a time, even after all that waiting. As a result, the potential investors loiter around, bored out of their minds. They don't have enough time to get a coffee or lunch, so they stand around and talk. And this boredom is your opportunity to get educated by some of the brightest and most experienced people in the field—for free!

If they are kind enough to share some details about their projects, take the time to drive to the properties they are working on and study the numbers. Once you have built a little rapport with them, ask them if they have room for more opportunities if you brought them an excellent one. No real estate investor in the world would say no to this question. And if you have no money, your first few opportunities are probably going to be some form of partnership anyway.

Go to a trustee sale tomorrow! It's like a kid who wants to play in the majors getting free first-base seats every day at Fenway. You will see who the players are, what they are buying, and how much they are paying. You'll have plenty of time to talk with them and ask them questions. They may even autograph your real estate binder if you ask nicely.

If you live far away from the county courthouse, start looking at fixers or low-end listings on Zillow, Craigslist, or any agent's MLS (Multiple Listing Service) feed on their website, and call the agents who are listing these properties.

Invite Someone to Lunch

The most powerful tool you have is the $30 sitting in your wallet or waiting on your credit card right now. Ask an investor from the courthouse or a Realtor you'd like to get to know better to lunch. Everyone loves a free lunch. When you buy them a $15 salad, you will be amazed at how much information they will give you.

While there may be some people who are threatened by this or reluctant to share, most people believe in mutual success. No one wants to do it all alone. If they see something in you that they like, they understand that you might make them money or become a useful resource for them as well. Build a win-win career. If you can make these people more money or bring them more opportunities, the odds are that they will bring you along for the ride.

When you take real estate agents to lunch, you magically become a viable client, even if you aren't one yet. You may have no money and even less experience, but now you are no longer just a faceless voice on the phone; you have become a doer, even by the simple act of dressing in some decent clothes, having a real conversation, and picking up a lunch tab. Trust us, that is more than most of their clients have done for them in the last 20 years.

Try to ask meaningful questions and actually listen to the answers. And have some tact. If you're talking with investors, don't ask, "How much did you make on your last deal?" but rather, "Have you had any projects that you were very proud of this year? What was it about that house or your approach that made it work out so well? Have you had any terrible evictions? How did you get the previous owners or tenants out?" People like to tell stories about themselves, so let them. Don't interrupt. You don't have a lot of meaningful insight to offer, so be polite and listen, and you might learn something. By building relationships, those agents might start calling you first when they come across opportunities, or they might even know hard money lenders you can talk to.

Investors will feel more comfortable and will be more willing to fund or partner on your next project if they know who you are. You might discover that you have something other than real estate in common. Maybe you're an avid golfer, musician, or fossil hunter, and you find out that you have a shared interest. Now perhaps you have a new friend and a potential partner. We're not saying this to be corny or silly; we're sharing this because people invest their time and money with people they like and trust, usually in that order.

Terence

I have never had one of my investors ask to see a bank statement or a financial statement. Think about that for a minute. They have bankrolled millions of dollars in real estate purchases and never seen my bank statement, credit report, or financial statement. Thank God they never did when they first started working with me, or they might have run the other way. They invested with me partially on the strength of the opportunities I brought, but even more on their knowledge of who I was as a person. My favorite lenders have known me since I was 12 years old, and that is what they are investing in. That makes them feel much safer than Wall Street or putting their money out with someone they have just met. Several of my other investor partners had only known me for a few months from interactions at trustee sales when they decided to put up their money and partner with me on our first projects.

While planning is important, you do have to take action as well. I had a plan, I knew how I wanted to build and grow my business, but my actual business grew by me working to find opportunities and nurture relationships and then asking the right people for the business.

I have also been good at adjusting quickly to failure. My most prolific partners became partners because they turned me down when I asked them to loan on my projects. They didn't want to make 10% or 12% when they could have the chance to make much more as partners. We have now done more than 25 properties together under this arrangement. Later I discuss how I might have made more money if they would have just done the loans, but notice that I didn't just give up when they said no.

Join a Real Estate Club

Next, join a local real estate club. Just like you get to know the players by going to the courthouse steps, if you find a good club with a varied membership, you will get to know the hard money lenders, the contractors, the people who do creative financing, and the real estate agents who people enjoy working with.

More importantly, you might learn about the contractors, real estate agents, and hard money lenders you should stay away from. Beware of gossip and petty rivalries, but listen closely to facts. If an investor tells you, "Don't partner with Joe; he's a dirtbag," that might just be jealousy, a past personal conflict, or maybe Joe is dating his ex-wife. But if he tells you, "Joe and I did a project, and he overpaid his sons to do the work, paid a full commission to his Realtor aunt to sell it, and left five subcontractors unpaid at the end," you might want to listen.

You can't put a dollar amount on how much you can learn, so find a real estate investment club. If there isn't one in your area, then start one. Put an ad on Craigslist saying something along the lines of, "Starting a local real estate investment club. We meet on Tuesdays at 6:00." All of a sudden, you will find like-minded people with similar interests, which will springboard your investing career in real estate.

Go to Our Website

Lastly, go to our website. We have spent the last 20 years accumulating an enormous amount of knowledge in many different areas of real estate, and we can't fit all of it into this book. On our website, there are videos, worksheets, and tools that will help you see if an opportunity pencils or not, how to structure your partnerships and loans, and more best practices for finding opportunities, completing renovations, solving problems, and getting projects sold successfully.

You will also find an extremely helpful and timesaving *Agent Screening Tool* that will help you find real estate agents in your market who understand the unique needs of real estate investors. This could be the most critical component of your business because the most expensive thing you can run into in investing is an agent who does not understand anything below retail. That is where the money is made. In most of the projects we have done in the last 20 years, we have made our money when we bought the property. Yes, we may have added value, but the real profit came from the initial under-market purchase. It's critical to find a real estate agent who understands that, and we put them through a screening process for you. We have already asked them the right questions to ensure they are solid matches for our clients. This feature alone will save you tons of time, stress, and wasted effort, and hopefully, it will make you a lot of money.

So get your feet wet and start looking at opportunities. Pick up the paper, go to a trustee sale, and start meeting people, and when they ask what you do, be honest. Say, "I'm a real estate investor. I'm new to the game. I'm just here watching." Most people want you to do well and want to share information. Some of the best information we ever received was because we bought a guy a chocolate milkshake. Ask Jerry about this story when you see him. Have fun, and we'll see you in the next chapter.

CHAPTER 3

THE PLAN

The words *planning* and *budgeting* will cause most people to go into a short spasm of anxiety. You would probably rather help someone move on Super Bowl Sunday than sit down and make a budget or a plan, even though that budget or plan could make you an extra $100,000 in the next year and every year after. Now, why is that?

For most people, when they make a plan or budget, it feels permanent. And sticking to the plan or the budget takes them into the realm of the unknown. "What if I mess up? What if I'm wrong? What if I fail?" But who cares if you fail! *Most of us have failed our way into success.* Think about it: Were you a failure walking? Yes, you were a total failure. You would stand up, and you would fall down, and it would hurt, and you would cry. Then you would stand up and fall down over and over again—until the one day you didn't. And then you weren't a failure anymore. And you walked fine, and then you ran, and then you danced, which was when the real fun started! The only real failure is to give up.

It's the same thing with success—you must fail your way into it. Most people want it to be perfect. But there is no perfect. Your first budget is not going to be perfect. Your first plan is not going to be perfect. And that is okay. Stop waiting for perfection and start looking forward to failing your way to what you want—more money, more time, and more freedom. Look at failure as the process that leads to success. A jet doesn't fly in a straight line from point A to point B; it is constantly course correcting, and that is what you must do when you make a plan, a budget, or a goal list. That which is not measured will not be gained.

Jerry

I know people who make goal lists once a year and then never look at them again until the next year, when they make new goal lists or the same goal list. Keep your goal list out where you can see it. Print it out in multiple places. Make a small version and laminate it for your wallet or purse. That way, it is always with you, reminding you of *why* you are doing it.

I have had a version of my goal list tucked in my wallet for over 10 years. It is right next to a picture of my kids. Again, be an example and not a warning for your future, for your family, and for your friends.

You may have heard it said, "What could you do if you could not fail?" We look at it a little differently. We ask, what if you *didn't care* if you failed? If you began thinking of failures as stepping-stones to what you truly want in life, then they are just temporary challenges, not permanent roadblocks. They are not failures anymore. There is a difference in the psychology just in that verbiage alone. Stop looking at things as failures and start looking at them as learning and growth challenges. Most of us love a good challenge.

Set up the rules in your favor so that you win. Have you ever thought about doing that? You probably have rules in your life that say for you to win, or succeed, or be able to relax, you must meet certain goals. Most of us do. Well, it is time to look at those rules and rewrite them so that you make it easier on you. To make $1 million, you must make $1 first. You can do it in a ton of different ways. To lose 15 pounds, you must lose the first pound and then the second. It doesn't mean you will lose a pound every day; it means you eat healthy most days, you exercise a little every day, and then, two months down the road, you have not only lost the weight, but you have also changed the reason the weight was there in the first place. You changed your plan, and you got a different result. As our Aussie friends say, good on you!

Get Excited About Your Plan

How do you get excited about creating your plan? It's different for everyone.

Jerry

For me it's simple. I have been drinking tea since I was four years old. You would think I was born in England, not Las Vegas. Whenever I do anything, I start off with a cup of tea. That immediately puts me in the right state of mind. Then I rub my hands together, and I smile or smirk. Terence and I smile and smirk a lot. And we laugh. It's not just because we have known each other for 40 years; it's because we have a lot of fun—with real estate and almost everything we do. That is the space you want to be in when you start off. A place of excitement, possibility, and joy!

Think of it like this: What is the great thing about the lottery? The great thing about the lottery is that for just a dollar, you get to dream about having millions or billions of dollars in your hand. You get to think of all the things you can do with the money. For one buck!

The fact is that you never even had to spend the dollar because you already had that dream of spending all that money. You just purchased the ticket so you could make it okay to dream. That is the state you want to be in when you sit down to put together a plan. You want it to be light. You want it to be fun. You want to be able to have a good time with your plan because it's about all the things you want. It's all the extra time. It's all the extra money. It's all the extra freedom. It's all the extra security. Everything you want will come from the plan. If you keep that in mind, you will stay in the pleasure zone and not the pain zone. It will start making things clearer for you, and clarity is power. That is super important and maybe worth writing down somewhere so you can see it every day: "Clarity is *power*."

Identify Your Resources

Before you start making your plan, you must identify your resources. Do you have money? Do you have even a little money to work with? Do you have time? Do you have an opportunity or opportunities that you can take to people who do have money even if you don't? If you know someone with money, and you can find an opportunity, then you can put a plan together.

Next, do you have good credit? Could you use your credit and somebody else's money to buy a property that comes up? Absolutely. We have done that. Can you leverage your experience and time and someone else's money? Absolutely! We have done it for over 15 years.

Do you have knowledge? Do you have knowledge of something that could be an asset to somebody else? If you have expertise in a field, then you can get paid for that in real estate. If you have special skills, write them down among your resources before you make your plan.

Develop Resourcefulness

Now you have identified your resources. So now you need resourcefulness. You have to believe that you have more than you need. "I have enough already. I have the resourcefulness to make use of these resources, or find those resources if I don't already have them." It will build over time like a muscle. If you want to be in shape, you can't just go running once. You must work these muscles continuously. The more you do it, the more you push through it, and the more you will know where you need to go.

Initially, you will most likely need to come up with a cash-flow strategy. Once you have enough cash to pay for your lifestyle, you can move to the wealth strategy. And that should be most investors' plans. If you already have $100 million, chances are you have this dialed in. But if you only have a little, then you need to get your cash flow covered first so that you can start accumulating the properties that will create wealth for you and your family for generations to come.

Map Out Your Plan and Team

Now it's time to get a yellow tablet or a sheet of butcher paper and map out your plan and your team. Remember to get in a great state before you do it. Rub those hands together, have a cup of tea, or imagine all the freedom that this will bring to your future life. And we mean map it out; put yourself in a circle, and start drawing in the members of your team and what their functions will be. It might be just you, it might be you and your spouse, or it might be you and nine of your friends and family members.

If you have a big team, for example, your uncle is an experienced contractor, your aunt is a Realtor, your sister is the world's greatest bookkeeper, and you have management experience at Barnes & Noble, then by all means make a detailed business plan with executive summaries and resumes for every member, a detailed breakdown of how you analyze properties, minimum profits and equity, and the interest rate you are willing to pay or portion of equity you are willing to share. Then get this plan in front of some of those hard money lenders you have met at the courthouse.

The 10 Components of Every Plan

While your plan depends on your strengths and interests, every plan needs to include these same components:

1. The Deal
2. The Money
3. The Terms
4. The Escrow Part I
5. The Rehab
6. The Sale
7. The Escrow Part II
8. The Back-Office
9. Repeat 100 Times/The System
10. Relax, Retire, or Relinquish

Again, within these components, there can be vast differences, but everyone is going through some version of this same linear process. In some rare cases, you might be able to skip one or more of these components. For example, if you wholesale some great properties, you would complete all the steps except the rehab. If you are able to assign the contract without closing escrow, you could omit components 2, 3, 4, 5, and 7, but you would still need 1, 6, 8, 9, and, of course, 10.

To start with, though, you must master components 1 through 8. Some say mastery takes doing something 10,000 times, or for 10,000 hours, but for our purposes, we believe you can cut that learning curve by at least half or even more. Just kidding. You will without a doubt master The Deal since you will be analyzing 10 to 20 properties per week, sometimes even more. In a larger market, you might weed through 50 to 100 possible properties per week, so true mastery might come within just a couple years or even less for this part of the process.

Let's take a very cursory look at each component, so you can start to understand the flow and see how basic this business can be when you're working with a plan. The following chapters will break each component down into each of its little working pieces, but if you can understand the overall process, it will serve as a clear road map, and you will always know where you are within every one of your projects and what you need to accomplish next.

1. The Deal. This part is exactly what it sounds like—finding possible opportunities and analyzing their potential. Ten flippers might have a hundred different ways of finding properties, but everyone must analyze them in a similar way. In some ways, it's simple math, but there can be forks in the road or different strategies or equations for analyzing the same house. The analysis is to try to find the quickest and most profitable route.

2. The Money. If you have a great job, lots of savings, and perfect credit, this part of the process may be as simple as talking to a mortgage broker or creating a plan with a loan officer at one of your local banks. If you're self-employed or have poor credit and none of your own money to start with, then you will go the private money or partnership route. We have talked a little about how to find these lenders and partners, and we will cover it in much more detail in Chapter 5, The Money. The seed we want to plant for now is that part of your skill will become matching the right lenders or partners with the right projects.

What we also want you to think about for now is that the money is the driving force of your business. The more capital you have access to, the more opportunities you can make. More importantly, you will never miss a great opportunity if you always have money lined up and ready to go. Most flippers settle on one or two lenders or partners and spend maybe 1% of their work time on finding money. If you can scale this up to even 5% of your working time, you will create many more options for success.

3. The Terms. Most of your contracts will have similar terms. Especially if you buy a lot of bank-owned properties or short sales, the asset managers have fairly strict guidelines they follow. But for some owner-financed or other creative deals, there are certain ways to structure your offer that will give the best benefit. We will train you to watch for those opportunities.

4. The Escrow Part I. A critically important, but often unsung hero of your business is your escrow officer. In Chapter 7, The Escrow Part I, we will teach you the qualities to look for in your escrow officer and how to get the most out of this relationship. Many escrow officers cringe when they work with flippers because we throw them curveballs they don't deal with in their day-to-day business. So the more you can do to pick the right person, the less resistance you will encounter.

This escrow period is also a great time for reflection and re-analyzing the opportunity. You must stay sharp and disciplined during this time because it is your window to escape if you find major issues. In some instances, this is also a great time to sweeten the opportunity by renegotiating for credits or finding a lender or partner who might give you a lower rate or a greater percentage of profits. Your escrow should be your sanctuary—a safe time to have the property tied up and the freedom to tweak the opportunity without the fear of losing it to a competitor. Don't waste your escrow period!

5. The Rehab. This is the make or break of your business. With the right contractor or team of subcontractors, you can rule the world. With the wrong team, it will take you much longer to rule the block, let alone the world. We will teach you all the planning and systems you need to keep your rehab team on point and make your rehabs nearly automatic.

Unless this is your core strength, the goal is to spend as little time coordinating rehab and wandering the aisles of The Home Depot as possible. Your time is $200 or more per hour, so you should spend the bulk of it finding opportunities and money. Yes, we think you are worth $200 an hour or more. How do you like them apples? The closer you can get to that or more, the better.

You must be smart about your rehab, and you have to be direct and inspire the contractors. Remember, they are contractors working on a budget. Don't expect them to be designers, visionaries, or real estate geniuses like you. You must guide them and give them a clear plan with easy-to-follow instructions. You will learn how to do this in Chapter 8, The Rehab.

6. The Sale. This is another area where many flippers lose focus. Just like you can't turn your rehab over to a contractor without a clear plan, you can't turn the sale over to a real estate agent and walk away. Agents work on spec, meaning it's a speculative business where they never know which buyer or seller is going to become a paying customer. Because of this, they are always juggling 20 balls and dropping most of them. Don't judge them too harshly; just understand it and be prepared to work with them through the process.

After you read Chapters 9 and 10, whether you're an agent yourself or planning to use a Realtor to sell your properties, you will have a massive arsenal of new ideas and strategies to help you create effective marketing and sales plans for all your projects.

7. The Escrow Part II. Here you must remember our approach to Escrow Part I and be prepared to enter the bizarro version. We want you to have a system to keep the buyers from using this time as their sanctuary and make sure they don't use their escrow to try to sweeten the opportunity for themselves. If you properly prepare for this stage of the process, you will be able to move them through it with the least amount of second-guessing, canceled escrows, wasted time, extra costs, unnecessary repairs, and uncertainty.

8. The Back-Office. Start your business with a strong back-office system of filing, bookkeeping, tax planning, transaction coordinating, and communication. It is very difficult to create this once you're in motion. In Chapter 12, The Back-Office, we will show you a system that works and help you build your most effective team.

9. Repeat 100 Times or The System. If you have followed the system for components 1 through 8, this should become an almost unconscious process, and with the stresses and uncertainties eliminated, it's a lot of fun. With the right team and colleagues, you will look forward to every lunch meeting, Starbucks planning session, and job site conference. And that is the whole point—to enjoy what you do.

Terence

I always appreciate my business when I encounter bank tellers, escrow officers, or other employees who tell me "Thank God it's Friday." I'm sitting there thinking, oh no, it's Friday; I wish I had more days in the week to work and get things done. I'm thinking this because I'm interested and challenged by my work. I adore my kids and love spending time with them, but I also love sitting at my computer, looking for projects, or walking through trashed houses and imagining what they could become. That's what life is supposed to be—one of endless possibilities.

Circling back to the lottery analogy, a little while back when the PowerBall surged to over $1 billion, I ran out to buy some tickets, something I never do. After all, I get that same rush every day when

> I make an offer, but the thought of $1 billion was exciting, so I went and bought 10 tickets.
>
> Now, the funny thing was that on the drive back to my house I started imagining winning the billion dollars, and as silly as it sounds, I started to worry about winning. I thought if I win a billion, I won't need to do any of this anymore, and that scared and disappointed me. I love the challenge of what I do and figuring out new ways to do it more successfully. You hear about all these people who win the lottery and quit their job the next day, and I think that is sad. We should all be so lucky to be doing something we would hate to lose.

10. Relax, Retire, or Relinquish. If you do this right, you will never want to retire. Some of the lenders and partners we work with are in their 70s and 80s and still love doing what they do. Why would you retire from something you love? We will also talk more about how to build a system for more passive income—if you want to live more of the Jer life.

That's all there is to it. Obviously, it's a lot to learn if you have never been in the business, but we are going to make it simple—maybe not easy, but simple. And by saving you from making every mistake we have ever made, you will get there a lot faster than we did.

Back to the task at hand, as Vizzini said in *The Princess Bride*, "Always go back to the beginning." Get in whatever state you need. Rub your hands together. Make a cup of tea. Get the fingers on the keys, the pencil on the paper, and go. Imagine you are talking to yourself in 5 years, telling yourself the story about how you started your successful real estate business.

A Note About The System

Throughout the book, when we mention "The System," we are referring to three different, but interconnected components. The first component is the basic system of acquiring real estate below market value, adding value through renovation, and reselling for profit.

The "system" also describes our philosophical viewpoint that a successful real estate business can be built by following a win-win approach that enriches not just the principals, but all participants including contractors, subcontractors, lenders, insurance agents, title and escrow officers, real estate agents, and most importantly, the homeowners who ultimately buy the properties and make everything possible.

Finally, the "system" is the template for planning and organizing your business. This is the system that will be hand-tailored by you to fit your team and your ideal business model. So in this sense, the system is *you*. A friend of ours who after 20 years of listening to Michael Jackson, was suddenly dumbfounded when he realized, "The Man in the Mirror…is me." In a similar way, the system is you. It's the pieces you take from this book and modify to fit your own market, team, experience, ambition, and lifestyle.

If you were becoming a schoolteacher, you couldn't hope that one book would give you all the answers. A great book might describe the best practices of teaching in general, it would hopefully promote positivity and compassion toward students, and it might give you some insights and anecdotes on what successful teachers have done in their own classrooms. But ultimately, if you're a fifth-grade resource teacher in inner-city Baltimore or a kindergarten teacher in rural California, the way you incorporate those practices into your own classroom is going to be very different. This is where we hope you will take these best practices and examples and apply them to your own business.

Because everyone's business is different, we do offer one-on-one training to help with the tailoring of the system to fit your needs and goals. Visit our website for more details: www.flippingmainstreet.com.

CHAPTER 4

THE DEAL

Terence

A few years ago I had an opportunity where I purchased a property for $102,000. It was a major fixer I thought would be worth $195,000 when I finished it. Early on, during a very rainy January, I tried to wholesale it for $135,000, but got no takers or even any interest – except one offer for less than I had paid for it!

The more I studied the offer, the more I began to see that there was a real shortage of updated country properties in my market. So I decided to increase my rehab budget and go for a top-of-the-market price by installing high-end finishes, a $4,500 fireplace insert (which I bought for $800 on Craigslist), and more. Ultimately, I spent $74,000 on the rehab, one of my highest ever. The project netted $47,000 in profit and became a house I was very proud of.

For me, there were three different paths I could have taken for this one project: wholesale, medium rehab, and high-end rehab. Another investor might have done his own work, gone super basic, spent $15,000 on simple fixes, sold it for $159,900 quickly, and moved on. There might have been four ways or 10 ways to analyze this one project.

You always have options and can recalibrate your strategy if needed. When you initially analyze the property, I recommend keeping it simple and planning your rehab and numbers to match the greatest number of comparable sales for the best odds of success.

Play to Your Strengths and Advantages

If you are the contractor, or you are going to do the bulk of the work, this might be where you make a premium. You probably wouldn't consider wholesaling a project when you can make money on both the property and profit on your work. If you're not an agent or a contractor, and you have an opportunity to wholesale a property without commissions or doing any work, this might be your most profitable path. If you know your market very well, are great with design, and love to shop for fixtures, you can go for the high-end rehab and capture the top dollar and top profits for your project. If you have a fast, organized, and reasonable contractor and a great discount agent, you can do the basic rehab and get in and out of the project in 90 days.

We are not trying to overwhelm you with options. Our emphasis is that you need to know who you are and which parts of this process are the most efficient for you and your team. If you have a low-end, slapdash contractor, and you try to use him for a high-end rehab, it's going to be a problem. If you are the contractor, but you're very slow and work alone, you might not want to take on a massive rehab where every component needs to get done, and it's going to take you eight months to complete. Know your strengths, and know your leverage. Better to make a fast $15,000 on a project and do 10 of these in a year than to make $30,000 on a project that takes you six months of hard labor and you can barely manage two per year. You'd be better off working for someone else.

Once you know who you are and your fastest path to profit, you can start analyzing opportunities under the template of your own strategy.

Know What to Look for

So how do you identify great opportunities? This is the question everyone asks. Even 10-year veterans come to us asking, "How are you finding your deals?" If you're out there looking, and you know who you are, the opportunity of a lifetime comes along about every three weeks. A more basic, workable project is probably out there almost every day, depending on the size of your market.

When you look for opportunities, look for anomalies. If there are 10 houses for sale in a neighborhood, and they are all in the $200,000s, look for the house in the high $100,000s where they might take $150,000. Or if three of the 10 houses are listed as fixer uppers, try to find the one that just needs carpet, paint, and cleaning. Or if they are all in the low $200,000s, but they are all under 1,400 square feet with single garages, and you find one that is 1,700 square feet with a double garage, that is the one to go after. Look for the anomalies.

You also have to push to create your own pricing anomalies by making lots of offers. If four houses are priced at $229,900, and you find the larger ones that need less work at $219,900, you need to find three houses like this and write three low offers until someone takes $190,000 or less for one you think you could sell for $274,500 to $279,900 if properly renovated for $30,000 or less.

Jerry

One of my favorite things to find is a home on two lots or a lot that is zoned as a duplex or triplex. This means I have many options if I do a rehab, and if I decide to own it for the future, I can split the lot or build two homes on it and double the income. I did this in Costa Rica and bought two lots that I split into four. I doubled my money by selling two lots, and then I still had two lots to do whatever I wanted. That's winning.

Arithmetic Versus Algebra

We always want to use arithmetic. We only want to go into opportunities where we know all the numbers on the front end.

Terence

I recently served on a panel put together by a large developer to determine the viability of a massive residential project. It was amazing to see a group of seasoned real estate veterans supporting a project with absolutely no numbers to work with.

> In a separate meeting with one of the principals, I explained that they were trying to project revenues on a project where they didn't know the future sales prices for the homes, they didn't know the costs to develop each lot, they didn't know the potential rental rates for the small commercial portion of the property, they didn't know the absorption or sales rate for the homes, and they didn't know how long it would take to get the project approved. It's hard to figure out $A + B + C + Y = Z$ when you don't have a single value to start with.

When you know your market inside and out, know your comps (comparable sales), know your construction costs, know your holding costs and sales costs, and know how much profit you need to make a project viable, then it's very easy to figure out how much you can afford to pay to acquire a property.

If you are just starting out and don't know how much it costs for five gallons of paint, a square of roofing material, or a yard of carpet, the good news is that you can figure it out in about two hours. Get dressed, drive to The Home Depot, and with a yellow tablet or your iPad in hand, start pricing basic materials and build a list, so you know the cost of everything from a bathroom vanity to a yard of mulch or a 20-foot roll of irrigation line.

Find out how much journeyman tradespeople are making in your market. If they are making $20 per hour, it costs the contractor about $25 per hour after taxes and withholdings. So if two painters can paint the inside and outside of a 1,300-square-foot house in four days, with $800 worth of paint and $200 worth of prep materials, you know it costs your painting contractor about $2,400 for that job. If he bids it at $3,400 or less, that sounds like a fair offer if you're going to give him five to ten projects a year. If he bids it at $6,000, he is making far too much money, and you need to find a new painter. Eventually, you will be so great at this, you will know the cost per square foot to paint the interior and exterior of a home even if there are vaulted ceilings and crown molding, down to the tenth of a cent.

While there will always be exceptions, you will eventually have a spreadsheet for your market with the dollar-per-square-foot costs for every component, so you can bid your projects and keep your contractors in check. If you and your brother-in-law partner love to paint and don't mind washing out the paint sprayer, your cost for this job with a veteran's discount at The Home Depot or Lowes is less than $1,000 plus your time and effort.

Terence

I regularly compete against a family group that has their own laborers in the family, their own staging furniture, a member who is a broker and attorney, and parents who handle all the shopping, cleaning, planning, and bookkeeping. It is very tough to outbid them because they are buying work for their family members and still making profits. They also use their own cash, so they have no external interest costs. A project I might consider minimal or breakeven might have $25,000 in profits and wages to their family members. If you have a great family or group of partners with varied talents, you will become unstoppable.

The only weakness of the group that I compete with is their creativity and ability to find properties. They have mastered only one source for opportunities, which is the courthouse steps for trustee sales, so when those are slow or unavailable, they end up sitting idle. By focusing so much internally, they also limit their volume because they aren't leveraging other people's time and labor.

If they would use contractors for some of the more profitable contracts and use their own team for the leaner ones, they could probably quadruple their production. They could also expand their business if they drew in some outside investors. They have an incredible track record, and investors would line up to partner with them, but they typically use only their own cash and a small credit line. I have watched them miss opportunities because they are waiting for their existing inventory to sell yet all their workers are sitting idle.

Every configuration has weak points, but our goal is to help you eliminate as many of these weaknesses as possible so you can reach your maximum potential.

Jerry

You should also have a contingency in your budget because surprises along the way will chew it up. If you make a conservative budget for your rehab, then add that to your budget price so that you don't end up losing money. After all, the goal is to get more money so you can enjoy more of life and spend more time with your kids and spouse, travel the world, and do more of the things you love to do.

A rule of thumb I go by for rehabs is to add a full 30%. So if you buy a house for $100,000, and you have a $50,000 rehab budget, add $15,000, which is 30% of the $50,000 rehab, and you are at $165,000 plus all your other costs and anticipated profit. If your comps show that your projected list price makes sense at those numbers, then go ahead and do the project. If it won't, or it's close, and you are just hoping that the market will go up between the time you buy it and the time you sell it, then you are probably going to lose money. So make sure you do your homework in advance.

If you don't buy the property right, it will show up in your rehab. It will cost more money and take longer than you anticipated.

Set Up an Agent Network

Since you have now done your research, and you know who you are—what your strengths are and what your costs are—now it's time to find some great opportunities. Where do you look? This question has launched a thousand books, seminars, and infomercials, but the answer is really very easy. Just remember: Opportunities are people. Huh? Every scenario you can think of that necessitates a sale, especially a distressed or discounted sale, involves people. Retirement, moving for a job, be closer to kids, getting married, divorce, death, job loss, bad tenants, foreclosure, or short sale—there are people at the core of all these situations. So if you're trying to find opportunities, doesn't it make sense to talk to people and to make sure people know that you buy houses? This will become the heart of your business. With social media and email, it's very easy to keep a steady stream of information flowing that lets people know that you solve real estate problems, you buy houses, even and especially when they're ugly, destroyed, abandoned, or neglected.

Even after all these years, though, some of our greatest sources for finding properties are still Realtors and our local MLS, so this is still most likely your easiest place to start.

Most people know at least three real estate agents. If you don't know any, go back to Chapter 2 and figure out how to take a few local agents to coffee or lunch, or simply get on the phone and start a dialogue. Tell them you are looking for projects. If they come across anything that might pencil out, ask them if they can give you a call or email you the listing so you can drive by. Give them some basic parameters. For example, you might need something to be 25% below market to make sense. Don't tell them that you will probably offer another 10% or more below the asking price. While you're at it, call 10 more agents with different companies and tell them the same thing. The reason for this is that you're hoping to get a look at a listing before other investors see it on the MLS. If you have 10 to 12 agents keeping an eye out for you, your odds of getting a jump on a good deal without competition increase dramatically.

Keep this list of agents and their emails and cell phone numbers on your desk and make sure you stay in front of them. Call them every three to four weeks, and eventually, you will intersect with one of them on a day when they are about to put a new listing for a short sale, probate, trust, or distress sale on the market. They would much rather double-end that project with you, meaning that they get both the listing and selling (buyer) side of the property, than share that with another agent who brings a buyer.

Try to build relationships with agents who list at least 20 homes per year to increase your odds of success. The top-tier agents who are listing 50 or more homes are tougher to get in with because they already have lots of clients, and you are an anomaly—you take more time, are harder to find opportunities for, and don't fit into their system. It still makes sense to drop them an email or call, but it's the middle tier that produces the best results.

You might also luck out and find those rare dealmaker agents who will dedicate their lives to finding you 10 great opportunities per year. Ask agents who the top short sale and REO agents in their office are. If you can build a relationship with agents who list 20 or more short sales per year, why wouldn't they submit offers for you on every decent one they list? You probably wonder why they don't do those opportunities for themselves since they're so good at finding them. It may be low self-esteem, lack of confidence, worry, or fear of failure. Regardless, these agents exist, and if you do get connected with one of them, make it easy for them. If they bring you good opportunities, don't beat them up excessively on commissions. You should get some kind of volume discount, but if you shave them down to nothing, they will find another investor, or they might finally get the idea to do it on their own. Don't kill the goose that is laying golden eggs!

Facebook Marketplace, Craigslist, For Sale by Owner, Auctions, and Trustee Sales

Once you have set up your agent network, start looking at Facebook Marketplace, Craigslist, watch for For Sale by Owner signs, and search auction websites. This should be a weekly activity that takes less than 10 minutes, but you must do it every week; for Craigslist maybe even every day or two. It is very low producing, but we have gotten opportunities from all these sources.

Agents hate working with auctions. They don't understand how they work, the paperwork doesn't match what their brokers require for their files, and they worry they won't be paid, or if they do get paid, it will be a heavily discounted commission. This makes auctions a great source of opportunities with limited competition, but they are still a long shot.

Terence

I make offers on almost 10 properties for every property I get through online auctions, but that still means I get two to three a year from this source, and I'm in a small county. If you're in a county or metro area with more than 200,000 people, you should be able to double that volume just from this one source.

I just picked up a great property from an online auction website. I was the high bidder in the sale, but my bid didn't meet their reserve, so after having to submit an offer higher than my winning bid, I still got a great property, far below what would have been available on the MLS.

If you have cash—the ability to load your pockets with cashier's checks kind of cash—you can venture into trustee sales at your local courthouse. You will have no guidance or second chances here, so we would advise against choosing this as your first option if you are not an experienced real estate investor. Get your feet wet with five to 10 properties before you consider this option. You will need title and legal assistance, you will need to understand tenant's rights and evictions, and you will often be buying properties without even seeing the inside of the house. Take an intensive trustee sale course before venturing down this road. You can take ours by enrolling on our website: www. flippingmainstreet.com.

Extend Your Network

Make sure your friends, family, Facebook friends, and everyone you know are aware of what you do and know that you will always buy a great deal. We have had contractors, friends, clients, subcontractors, attorneys, and even competitors refer good properties to us. If you make the right investments, it doesn't take too many to make for a great year.

Jerry

When I was 23 years old, I lived in Austin, Texas, and worked as a bartender. I had the daytime shift, and every day at three o'clock, five or six people would come in and sit at my bar. One looked like he worked on a ranch; another looked like he worked in an office, and yet another had the appearance of a mechanic.

Over the next month, I learned that they were all multi-millionaires, and they owned a lot of real estate—hundreds of thousands of acres of land, commercial buildings, apartment buildings, and single-family homes. They would just come to my bar because they liked it. They would sit there and get loaded and just chat with each other.

I remember hearing conversations like, "Hey, do you guys know anybody who has 5,000 acres for sale? Because we're looking to do a deal in West Texas." One person would respond, "You should call Taylor; he has 5,000 acres that he has been trying to sell." I was blown away by the transactions that happened right in front of me among people who most observers would have discounted as drunks at a bar. They all dealt with real estate, and if they didn't have it, then they knew somebody who did.

It is imperative to be in the network rather than outside of the network. So tell everybody that you're in real estate and looking to invest. Then all of a sudden, the network will show up.

Study the people who are doing deals, and you will become one of them very quickly.

There are as many ways to find opportunities as there are people flipping houses, but if you just focus on any two of the strategies we just presented, you can find more projects than you can handle. Our hope is that we can help you get so good at finding opportunities that you can keep the exceptional ones for yourself and refer the more mediocre properites out to partners so you can still make a percentage and let someone else shoulder the time, effort, and risk. We also hope that by using our tools, you will be able to see the opportunities that other investors don't see. If you can do that, you will be able to build as big a flipping conglomerate as you want.

Understand the Cycles

It is also important to know where you are in the market cycle. Real estate, like any other investment tool, works in cycles. It doesn't always go up, and it doesn't always go down. Make sure you are aware of where you are in the cycle.

Jerry

When the cycle is going up, most of the rules don't apply. The first time I went snowboarding, there was 26 inches of fresh powder on the mountain. So I did what I do when I water ski; I leaned back. That was what I did the whole day. I didn't have to learn how to snowboard; I just leaned back and had the time of my life. That is what an up cycle is like. You can do no wrong. By the time you close the contract, it's worth 30% more than you bought it for. It's a magical time, and it doesn't happen often. You must be aware of it. You don't have to apply the rules; the opportunities just happen.

But as we learned in 2008, that is also a way to lose everything you own very quickly. In down cycles, you must look for the lowest hanging fruit. You must time everything, be quick, and watch the costs.

In an up cycle, people tend to go outside their comfort zones because they are excessively optimistic. Conversely, in a down cycle, people are not willing to go outside their comfort zones. That is when the location is crucial for your opportunities. You don't want your profit to go down, so you must be aware that location does play a massive role in a down cycle.

Jerry

When we were in the heart of the boom between 2002 and 2007, I had a rule for investment properties I purchased: When it made $100,000, I would sell it in one year and a day because the long-term capital gain would be 15%. It was a great rule at that time because that happened a lot. Now the rules are different in a down cycle and probably will be different in the next up cycle. You must constantly course correct your plan. Do this, and you will most likely be one of the successful investors in your group.

Learning where you are in the real estate cycle in your market is very easy. Ask your agents, talk to title people, talk to other investors, and do some research. Every town, city, and part of the country is different. Countries are different. The Chicago Board Options Exchange has a tool for evaluating cycles in the stock market called a Volatility Index or VIX. If you're doing your homework, talking with colleagues, and constantly looking at inventory and comparable sales, you should be able to create a Real Estate Volatility Index or "RE-VIX" for your market pretty easily.

You must set up proper systems (which we will cover in Chapter 13, Repeat 100 Times/The System), so that no matter whether you are in an up cycle or down cycle, you treat the opportunities the same. If you implement your systems in an up cycle, you will make more money than you ever imagined. If you stick to your system in a down cycle, you're going to make exactly the amount of money you wanted to make because you're adhering to your system, and you know the costs before you even enter the offer.

Know How to Operate in a Down Cycle

Terence

Recently, a new investor who is fairly inexperienced asked me nervously, "What happens if the market crashes? Would we keep going or just stop?"

The great news is that if you build a solid system and stay disciplined, your business will survive and even thrive during the next crash or recession.

I explained to this investor that my local market peaked in August of 2006, and while it seemed like it was an instant implosion at the time, it was gradual in a macro view. Prices were probably dropping by 1% to 1.5% per month from that peak.

The key factor, once you have identified that you are in a declining market, is to get ahead of the market immediately and reload. If you are carrying a house that you projected to sell at $225,000, and it's suddenly sitting, and you determine you are entering a down cycle, you need to cut your losses and recalibrate. You must get ahead of the competition and ahead of the market, which might mean making a 10% or greater decrease in your pricing *and* massively stepping up your marketing, commission bonuses, staging, maintenance, and detailing. Instead of making $30,000 on this house, you might make $3,000 or break even, but the first goal is to survive and be able to take advantage of the new declining market.

Now you survive, and you start to see a slew of new REO listings and short sales, so you start evaluating this with your same technique for analyzing properties, *but* you need to factor in the decline in the market. So if you project your numbers and estimate that a house is currently worth $225,000 in today's market, but it will take you three months of rehab and three months to sell it, you better adjust by 1.5% per month for those next six months and an extra two to three months for good measure, which means it still had better be profitable at $199,900. If you can't make that work, don't buy it.

The great news in a declining market is that if you can't find an opportunity one week, all you have to do is wait. Distress in a market becomes exponential, so two or three REOs and short sales in a neighborhood suddenly lead to five or 10 more. Be patient in a declining market and keep upping your game on the rehab.

During down cycles, you should be able to do rehabs for less money than in up cycles because your contractors and subcontractors are going to become more motivated and price competitive as the easy jobs dry up. In 2009, we could get a good-sized roofing job done for $5,000; now in 2021 it's nearly tripled. In 2009, they told us it was because oil prices were high. Now oil prices have dropped by 50%, and the roofing expense has almost doubled. What it really has to do with is the demand for work. Contractors are busy again, so they are not going to add a job to their schedule unless they can make a few thousand dollars in profit. Their costs for labor, materials, insurance, and rent have also gone up, so they must keep moving their prices up so they won't lose money. When we see the next downturn, all these costs will go down again, and sometime in the next few years, roofers will be willing to do a quality roof for $5,000 again.

When the market declines, you will see more opportunities for great properties, fewer competitors with the cash or credit to buy them, and lower costs for rehab. Just make sure to adjust your pricing accordingly and always stay ahead of the market. Don't try to catch a falling knife. Be cautious, don't over-leverage, and always be prepared for the worst-case scenario.

Several of our partners who operated heavily during the downturn were always in a strong cash position and were very stubborn. When they couldn't sell their flips for what they wanted in 2008 to 2012, they turned them into rentals. Starting in 2013, they began selling them off. A few that they sold in 2015 had gone up another 50% while tenants were paying the mortgages. We are not all in a position to maintain long-term holds like that, but if you can, it's another great tool for your down-market arsenal.

What Not to Do in an Up Cycle

Now you may think we are going to suggest the exact inverse for a rising market; that you can project your opportunities ahead by 1% to 1.5% per month to make them work. *Wrong!* Never buy on speculation or try to make your profit on the market instead of your expertise and hard work. Continue to run your analysis and buy properties based on current prices. If you finish a four-month rehab and find out that the value has jumped up by another $15,000 to $20,000, good for you. Take the money and move on to the next project. It's just like we talked about with arithmetic versus algebra; no one truly knows what the market is going to do tomorrow or next month or next year, so if you bet your entire livelihood on a great big unknown *X*, you had better think twice. The risk is too great. We are all for riding a market up, and we did it tremendously well from 2002 to 2006 and 2012 to 2021, but every property we bought was a huge value in real time on the day we bought it as well. You are working too hard and too intelligently to gamble with your success. We want you to have a lasting and low-stress business, so stay disciplined and only buy when the numbers make sense whether you are in an up or down cycle.

Open Up to the Opportunities

Your belief system is going to play a major role in whether opportunities pop up for you all the time or they never pop up at all. If you have the perspective of, "I never get any deals," then chances are you're right. But if you believe that opportunities are out there all the time, you will start seeing more of them. If you believe that you will do 50 projects this year, you will probably start tripping over properties every morning when you go out to get the paper. If you start believing that there are opportunities that will make you anywhere from $10,000 to $50,000 with a limited amount of your time, but a lot of leverage of other people's time, effort, and expertise, then that is what will happen.

We wouldn't be able to write this book, have a website, and have seminars on how to do these things if opportunities didn't exist. We are a testament to that. Great deals exist in every market, every day. We have found properties that we have made $50,000 and $100,000 on in a tiny, rural market. We have found these kinds of extraordinary deals not once, but many times. We didn't doubt them or second-guess them when they came along; we seized the opportunities and ran with them.

Sometimes when you get into something new, it's incredibly important to get a different perspective. If you are usually the pessimist, try to take the optimistic point of view. Try looking at things differently. Take a leap of faith with the attitude that this can work rather than thinking that it will never work. If you have that optimistic perspective, you will do better in the long run. The more you open up, the more opportunities will show themselves to you.

Jerry

I can spot a For Sale by Owner sign out of the corner of my eye through a shrub down a side street 300 yards away. I have a talent for it. When you start opening up to the fact that opportunities are everywhere and realize that for sale by owner properties can be some of the best, then you will start noticing these signs everywhere. Don't just notice them and drive by. Notice them and stop. Get the information off the sign. Call the number.

Every time I used to visit Redding, I would drive the street where I grew up. During one visit, I spotted a for sale by owner. I stopped, knocked on the door, and talked to the guy. He was an investor who had bought the house and wanted to flip it quickly, so he flipped it quickly to me.

I barely even cleaned it up. Within six months, I made over $40,000 on it. It was a phenomenal opportunity that took all of 20 minutes of my time to stop at and a couple of hours to get it cleaned up. Now that is an hourly rate I can live with.

You may wonder, "Well if this is such a great property, why am I going to get it for this low price, and how am I going to make any money on it?" That property might have been handed down from grandma and cost nothing. It might be that they just paid it off, or perhaps they bought it for $60,000, and now the market says it's $150,000. Perhaps getting out of it quickly and selling it for $100,000 is a win for the sellers because they want to move to Costa Rica and live on the beach. You never know. If it's a deal to you, don't worry about the story, just act on it.

When you find an opportunity, one of the most important things is to make a move quickly. Tie it up; get a contract written. Whatever you possibly can do, make sure you do it. If you make 100 offers, and you get 10, and each of these makes you $15,000 to $25,000, then that is $150,000 or more, and that is a solid income in most parts of the country. You can do more or fewer properties; it's up to you. That's the beauty of this business; you can structure it however you want and adjust it any time. If you decide you want to slow down a little one year, you can. If you come back from your three-month sabbatical and want to hit it hard and double or triple your production, you have all the tools and planning you need to do that. Only you know how much money you want to make.

Jerry

I used to follow a newsletter written by an investor in Los Angeles who flipped lots of houses. He had reached the point where he was tapped and couldn't load any more properties into his system. He didn't have any more hours—his contractors were too busy—but he kept sending the newsletter. Then, even if he was saying no to 80% of the properties thrown at him, he still had the option and didn't miss the best opportunities.

If you do it right, the opportunities will come from everywhere. You just have to be open to them, and when they get to you, make sure you act.

CHAPTER 5

THE MONEY

Maybe you have rich in-laws, or your best friend won the lottery, so you have no problem funding your flips. For the rest of us, finding the money is often the most critical part of the business. You can find 100 great opportunities, but if you can't come up with the money to buy them, complete the renovations, and pay the holding costs, those 100 opportunities won't make you a penny because you won't be buying them.

Friend and Family Lenders

Terence

Let me start the conversation about The Money by telling you how I lost a million dollars. Or, I should say, one of the times I've lost a million dollars. After clawing my way out of the Great Recession, I began expanding my flipping business. I partnered with a couple of my good friends and clients who could fund the projects I wanted to do. The proposal was very simple, and it is a great way to start. They put up all the money for the purchase, the renovation, and the holding costs. My job was to find the properties, coordinate all the renovations, pay all of the bills, market the homes (since I'm a licensed broker), and handle the escrows and paperwork on both the purchase and the resale transaction. At the end of the project, we split the profits 50/50, and there was no interest charged for the money. It's not a terrible prospect when you're starting out and much better than just getting commissions or not getting anything at all.

However, after about five years of doing properties this way, I received a call from a very close family friend who did a lot of hard money lending. He was calling to ask why I wasn't using him and his wife to fund my projects. He actually sounded a little upset that I hadn't been working with them. I sheepishly explained to him that because we had such a close relationship and since I had known him and his family from the time I was 12 years old, I didn't want to take the chance of hurting our friendship. He explained back to me that they didn't need me looking out for them; they had loaned against real estate for years and knew what they were doing. They felt like they would be benefiting by getting to work with someone they trusted. And they were also doing it because they wanted to help me grow my business and because they sincerely cared about my family and me. I was embarrassed but flattered and excited to start working with them.

I ran out and found a bank-owned house that I bought through an online auction for $146,599. I had told my friends/new lenders that I would happily pay 12% interest on the money since they had agreed to finance the acquisition and the rehab, and would even let me take my commission on the purchase at the closing. They had also agreed not to take any payments until the house had resold to keep my carrying costs down. Try getting that from your local bank. Now imagine my surprise when I showed up to sign the closing papers and found out that they had insisted on funding my project at 8% interest. I was floored and incredibly grateful.

I spent just under $40,000 on the renovation, and I used a great contractor who completed it quickly. The house really turned out well and sold quickly too. I purchased the house on August 28, and it closed escrow on the resale on November 15 after a fairly extensive remodel that included a new roof, some new windows, flooring, moving walls, all new fixtures, etc. My lenders made about $3,800 in interest, and I made about $33,000 in profit on the flip as well as a $4,400 commission on the purchase. I worried that they would be upset that they had essentially taken the whole risk and had made one-tenth of the money that I had made. But were they upset? No. They were thrilled because it proved to them that they had made the right choice. It validated their decision to invest their money in me and my business. They loved that my projected numbers were correct, and the huge profit in the project made them feel that their money had been safe all along.

So how did I lose the million dollars, you wonder? It's all in the math. I had spent five years doing properties with partners and splitting profits instead of borrowing money from these trusted friends at 8%. Compare the results on this opportunity. Had I done the project with my usual partners, we would have split the profits, which would have been $36,800 with no interest, so $18,400 to me, plus my $4,400 commission for a total of $22,800. By partnering with my friends and paying 8% interest and keeping all the profits, I made $37,400—almost $15,000 extra on one property. I started going through all the projects I had done previously and calculating how much I had given away by not calling my friends sooner, and it was staggering. Even worse, I started to realize how many opportunities I had missed entirely because my partners could only do two to three houses at a time. The $1 million is probably a very low estimate.

Now consider that you have probably lost $1 million as well. What do I mean? Well, you may have the same friend or family member who would happily loan you the money or partner with you if you would simply present a viable plan and ask. My lender friends have less than 10% of their investment portfolio in the stock market because they feel the risk is too great. Instead, most of their money is out in private loans, typically in the 10%–12% range. In most cases, it is probably loaned out at less than 60% loan-to-value ratio and on loans that have a two to five-year term. So they might

> not be getting double-digit returns with me, but they are getting a far better return than they would with any CD or savings account. They also feel they have invested the money safely in their own community with someone they trust, and this portion of their portfolio stays fairly liquid since it's typically only out for three to six months at a time.
>
> I should also say that I did sign personal guarantees for the initial few loans because the loan-to-value ratio was essentially 100% plus the accrued interest, so I was taking an extra level of risk to put my new lenders at ease.

If you asked your grandparents very nicely over your next Sunday dinner, they might loan you the money at 4%, and they will be thrilled to get a better, safer return and help someone they love to grow their business. If you were in their situation, wouldn't you?

Now, you better know what you are doing before borrowing grandma's nest egg. If you lose it, you're going to ruin a lot of Christmases for everyone, so treat these investments a thousand times more carefully than if they were your own. You might be okay risking $100,000 on a flip, but they are trusting you, so you had better be trustworthy and make it work or be prepared to find a way to pay it back.

Other Partner Plan Alternatives

Okay, so what if you're a total loner with no family or friends and this kind of opportunity doesn't exist for you? Fine. Start with the partner plan we outlined at the beginning of the chapter. Offer to find all the opportunities, do all the work, and split the profits 50/50. On the first project, you might have to give them 70/30, but who cares? Who cares if it were 80/20 if it was the first building block in a multi-million-dollar career? It's all about creating a working relationship, and you can increase your percentage as you have more and more success.

Terence

As I mentioned earlier, I have one set of partners who I initially approached to lend me money for flips. They were much too shrewd for that and instead opted for the partnership arrangement, which has served them much better. I completed one flip with them that gave them an annualized return of over 100% on their investment. How? I flipped the house in 39 days, and we split $38,000 in profit. They had put out about $160,000, so they made $19,000 in 39 days—more than 11% return in just over one month, and I still made $19,000 plus a commission! Talk about win-win. This was an exceptionally fast opportunity, but I'm doing another one just like it as I write this. And yes, this time, it's with my 8% money.

You must adjust your plans to suit different partners with different needs and thresholds for risk. If I'm chasing a property that seems a little riskier, I have offered partners a 50/50 deal where they get their profits first, and I only get mine after they have made theirs.

In one case, I had found a house that I really believed in, but my partners were skeptical, and the dollar amount was a little higher than they would have liked, so they passed on the offer. It was a bank-owned house that had been bought by a wholesaler. There was a pool that was still covered over with safety mesh and tarping that was green with algae and full of frogs. I cut a hole through the plastic safety cover and could see that the former owner had recoated the pool with a beautiful Pebble Tec finish still in perfect condition. I talked to the neighbor, and he confirmed that the old owner had spent over $20,000 on that pool only two years before losing the house. It was probably the main reason why he had lost the house!

I knew the house was a winner, so I went back to my money partners the next day and told them that they would get the first $25,000 in profits. If the project only made $25,000, I would make nothing. They looked at each other and nodded. They liked the idea and agreed to fund it.

I initially thought that house would make $40,000, so I was hoping to make $15,000 and spent the next month kicking myself that I hadn't offered them the first $20,000 instead of $25,000. However, the house came out better than expected and ended up making $58,000 in profit. My partners got $29,000, and I got $29,000—and my kids and I got to swim in that pool for two months during the renovation and escrow. The summer of 2014 was a good one!

Remember, you must adjust, so try to stay flexible, or you will miss opportunities. I have had many properties that I put in escrow with the intention of using one partner or lender, but then as I delved further into the numbers, I switched mid-escrow to another lender that was a better fit for the type of property or offered terms that made me more money. I might start out with my 8% lenders, but if I realize it's going to be a long, riskier flip, it might be worth spinning off to other partners so I don't have to lie awake worrying about interest piling up.

I don't recommend tying up properties or writing offers without a plan for how you are going to pay for the property, but I often tie up opportunities with the intent of using one of my private lenders, but if I see a better match during my escrow, I will often change at the last minute to a different lender. You can do this if you have multiple reliable lenders and partners. Never do this when you don't have any lenders or partners lined up, or you will quickly burn whatever bridges you have built in your local real estate community.

Every opportunity and every situation is different, so make sure you are willing to adapt. You will come up with scenarios that we might never have thought of. Just try to make it a win-win. Make sure that your lenders and partners are making money and that you find opportunities that are good enough to minimize their risk. If you can do this consistently, you won't need more than two or three partners and lenders to build a substantial business. If you screw it up and lose their money, you will be spending all your time replacing the good lenders and partners you lose. Be smart; do it once, do it right, and you will never have to pitch a lender again.

If you pitch your good friend who has a stable government job and a big retirement account invested in mutual funds, just be aware that he might not be capable of weathering the highs and lows of investing. He might not understand why escrows fall out or why you need more money to complete unexpected repairs. Adapt your presentation to match your audience; some potential investors will require more information and more contact throughout the process to feel that their investment is secure.

Start by approaching people who already invest in real estate. Some of our best partners are super savvy real estate investors and flippers who have done dozens of projects. In some cases, they are slowing down as they hit their 60s and 70s, so they love the idea of someone else doing the work, but they like staying busy and involved and making great returns. In other cases, they are successful flippers who are burned out on doing their own properties, but they want to leverage our knowledge and time, so they are willing to trade some of the profits to keep all their time for themselves.

Flipping can be a very lonely business. Flippers often work out of home offices without close colleagues, so suddenly the opportunity to partner and get some camaraderie with a like-minded partner is exciting to them.

Terence

I have several partners who have given up money to do a project with me simply because they are bored and want to work on something together. I have even done it in reverse by partnering with friends and colleagues when I haven't needed to. It's always great to see how someone else is doing it. And after all, if you don't enjoy yourself and enjoy the people you work with, you should probably be doing something else! Now go find some money!

Jerry

A couple of years ago, Terence and I were discussing how to find investors to help with flips. I suggested we write down every millionaire we knew personally in our hometown of Redding. Now, this is a small town of fewer than 100,000 people, but in that tiny market, we knew more than 50, and it didn't take us long to write the list. So all of a sudden, we realized that there was a ton of money out there, and people want more than the minuscule return they get in a savings account or money market account.

The people who make a lot of money but don't have the time to manage their investments themselves are people like doctors, dentists, and attorneys—professionals who spend 50 to 60 hours a week on their businesses. They are not actively going to look for real estate projects, so if you can come to them with opportunities that will make them a reasonable rate of return, they will be happy to loan you the money they have saved over the years. Look for those people you can do business with every day and ask them if they are interested in your opportunity. Most of them will be open to hearing about it as long as you have a plan.

As we mentioned earlier, most investors spend only 1% of their time or less soliciting lenders. If they get one, they typically rely on that lender and limit themselves to the number of projects that person can do. We encourage you to spend 3% to 5% of your time looking for new partners and lenders. Think of the massive difference over a career of paying 12% interest on the money plus points versus borrowing at 8% interest with no points. If you continued looking, could you find someone who would do it for 5%? You won't know unless you keep looking and asking. What costs us the most money in our lives is not asking—not asking for help, not asking for loans, not asking for partners, not asking for the sale, not asking for success! Start asking for everything today, and you will be shocked by how many people say *yes*!

If you feel like you can't ask for money, then find someone else in the real estate business who likes to do it. We have friends who love to find investment money, and they are great at it.

> ## Jerry
> When we were writing this chapter, I was sitting across from a woman who was on the phone, and her conversation went something like this: "Yeah, we're raising $2.1 million, and I already have $1 million."
>
> After she had gotten off the phone, I asked her, "What about raising money do you like?"
>
> She replied, "Well, whenever there is a worthy cause, people will always donate money."
>
> Sometimes, people getting a better return on their money is enough of a worthy goal. And having someone they trust or someone they see is hungry to better themself can be enough for them to go forward with the project.

Get Clear on Your Mindset

The biggest excuse for not having more money usually starts with, "If I had more money, I could make more money. If I had more money, it would be much easier for me to invest in real estate. If I had more money, I wouldn't have any problems." Saying this is a way of setting up a boundary to not take a risk and not be embarrassed by failing.

What do you think about money? Is it the root of all evil? Is it the answer to all your problems? Is it bad? Is it good? Is it indifferent?

At the end of this chapter, we have an exercise we would like you to do so that you can identify your belief system around money. So now, take a minute to get in touch with what you believe and what you think other people believe about money. It will help you wrap your head around the creative part of real estate, which is finding the money.

Your beliefs about money work at a subconscious level. If you believe that people with a lot of money are bad, it will hold you back because you might think you will turn into an evil person if you make a lot of money. On the other hand, if you believe that you can help people on a larger scale if you are wealthy, then you will look at making more money as a great thing. You will be able to help people, your family, your friends, and charities you believe in.

Jerry

I came from very modest means and wasn't raised with a lot of money. To me, money was neither the best thing in the world nor the root of all evil. It just existed around me.

When I bought my first piece of real estate, which was a condo in West Hollywood, I didn't have any savings, was massively in debt, and had two cars on my credit report. To get the loan I needed to buy the condo, I had to write a letter to the mortgage company, asking them to believe in me. I also had to have my ex-wife from whom my divorce wasn't finalized sign off that she wouldn't have any ownership interest in the condo. If I had looked at all these hurdles to get into my very first piece of real estate on paper, I probably wouldn't have done it. But I just believed that the money was going to flow and that I was going to get this. It was my first foray into real estate. It was also very successful; I more than quadrupled my money in that property, and I got to live in a great, safe neighborhood and meet people who are still some of my best friends today.

There is more money available right now than at any other time in history because two extremely wealthy groups of people—the World War II "Greatest Generation" and the oldest "Baby Boomers"—are transferring money down to their children. So there is a ton of money just sitting there, begging for you to find a place to put it. We talked about how you would find it, but how do you not?

Since your belief system on money is paramount, get your friends together and play Monopoly, The Game of Life, or Cash Flow. You will play the games the same way you play life, so in a couple of hours, you will learn more about the way you will invest in real life and get more clarity on your belief system on money than you ever will going out and trying to do it in the real world.

After you have gotten clear on how you value money and your belief system on money, get creative. Watch Ken Robinson's TED talk "Do Schools Kill Creativity?" Those 18 minutes on creativity could change where, how, who, and what your thoughts are and your belief system around money, and it may change the *why*. Once you identify your *why*, all the other pieces will fall into place easily.

So play some games and go out and talk to people. As soon as you get over your hump about money, then money is just a magnifier. If you are not a good person and you suddenly come into money, it will bring out that side of you. But if you're a good person, our hope is that more money is going to make you an even better person.

BELIEF SYSTEM EXERCISE

A belief system is how you feel about something with complete conviction. Now, this doesn't mean that it is true, but at this moment, it is true to you.

For example, you may have a belief that all cats meow. No one can convince you otherwise, until one day a cat comes up and barks at you. At first, you may not believe it, but then the cat barks at you again. Then you bring a friend over, and the cat barks at him, too. All of a sudden, your belief system about cats isn't as sturdy as it used to be. Belief systems can change with enough experience and supporting evidence of the new belief.

So what are some of your beliefs around money?

Print this exercise, write it out on a piece of paper, or cut and paste it into a document and fill it in. The important thing is that you do this now because your financial future depends on it!

Money equals _____ .

People with a lot of money got it by _____ .

Money can _____ .

Money will cause you _____ .

To get a lot of money, you must _____ .

Money has _____ .

There is _____ money.

Now look at your answers and think carefully about what you answered. This is important because you might have been carrying around this belief about money for years or even decades!

If your answers around money are mostly negative, then it's time to do a reframe. This is imperative because you will not attract money into your life if you believe it will destroy you or make you a horrible person.

Think about your answers above with a positive outlook. If money is so powerful that it can "ruin your life," then it can also change lives by providing food, education, or jobs to help less fortunate people.

If money can cause you to become a spoiled douchebag, then it can also fulfill your dream of creating a nonprofit that provides services for veterans, the disabled, sick children, or neglected animals.

Remember, money is a magnifier. If you are a thoughtful or giving person, then you will still be that with money. You will then be able to be more thoughtful and more giving to your family, your community, and your world.

CHAPTER 6

THE TERMS

Terence

A few years ago I found a deal on Craigslist that looked like a great project. It was an older home with a driveway that looked like a parking lot for shopping carts, there must have been at least a dozen and there wasn't a grocery store for miles. The home had obviously become a stopover point for the homeless. The roof had weeds growing between the shingles, and the trash and debris in and around the house was waist deep. It was perfect! And the seller was only asking $39,000. I was a little hesitant because the underlying zoning was office, but there were several other rental homes on the street, so I figured worst case I could keep it as a rental myself if that was easier than reselling it.

As I talked more with the 'seller' I learned that he wasn't actually the seller, he was the grandson of the elderly owner. He was also fresh out of a real estate seminar and the 'guru' was helping him structure this deal for grandma. She was an elderly woman who had been fighting cancer and because of her medical bills the house had fallen into ruin. The homeless people literally started showing up while she was still living there, because the house looked so terrible that even they assumed it was vacant. When the vagrants started coming around she got scared, so she moved out and was living with her sister. The would-be real estate expert and his guru were giving grandma $10,000 for the house so she could rent a new apartment. Now I had offered $34,500 and he accepted and was expecting to make a quick $20,000+ in a couple weeks. Wouldn't that have been nice? Unfortunately he had probably spent his $10,000 on the seminar, so he didn't have any money to get grandma into her new place. Instead, he proposed that I release the first $10,000 right away and once grandma got settled in her new place and 'got a few other issues resolved' we could fund the rest and close the escrow. I was more than a little reluctant to agree to this structure. I constantly take a lot of upfront risks when buying properties; I've risked and lost thousands of dollars over the years for inspections on properties that I didn't buy, but to risk $10,000 right out of the gate when there were lots of red flags and layers seemed like a terrible idea. Even if grandma agreed and it was disclosed to her that her grandson was going to instantly resell the house for $24,500 more than she was getting, any family member or decent local attorney would be ready to jump in after the fact and scream 'elder abuse' and I think they would be getting that $24,500 plus $15,000 in legal fees a year later, meanwhile tying up the house with a lis pendens (a legal action that prevents the property in litigation from being transferred until the legal matter is sorted out) while my interest meter ticked away at 12% a month on the $34,500 plus the other $50,000 in rehab I was going to put into the house. After I explained this to him, he got offended and said he would get his own private money to buy the house. I told him to let me know when he got it all figured out.

While this was all going on, I had one of my escrow officers rush a title report and we quickly saw that it was a disaster with multiple deceased parties on title, past tenancies in common, and other title issues which essentially meant that there were probably 2-3 other heirs who had an interest in the property, all of which wouldn't be resolved until someone paid the money to start a probate hearing on the estate, which could take years to resolve. What a mess.

I moved on to 8 other simpler projects, but happened to drive by the property a few weeks ago. The shopping carts are all still there and probably will be for years to come. This is another example to show that terms should make the deal more simple, not make the deal more complicated.

If you expect to make your first million in real estate by tricking little old ladies into weird double escrows that will take three phone calls to explain to your next buyer, then you desperately need to read this book. When you buy a bank-owned property, a short sale, or simply a distressed, trashed property from an overwhelmed owner, everything is transparent. Everyone involved knows that you are going to invest substantial time, money, and effort to earn your profit on the project. Then there is very little legal risk and no misunderstandings, which is how we like it. We are all for picking up great opportunities that some inept agent has underpriced or when people need a quick cash sale before they lose the house to the bank. But if you are looking for magical terms that will make you rich, go back to the beginning of this book and start over.

There are a few rare people who excel at "wholesaling" and spend their careers finding this kind of distress, but they still need the money or private financing to make the wheels spin. We don't profess to be experts at wholesaling; we are experts at buying, renovating, and re-selling for amazing profits where everyone gets value, and that is what we hope to teach you.

Terence

In my market, there are probably 20 to 30 active investors who are flipping two or more properties per year, all making a good living and some making a phenomenal living for this area. I know of only two "wholesalers" in my market, and neither one seems to make much of a living at all at wholesaling per se. We're not saying that wholesalers don't exist, or that they can't make a lot of money, but we are saying that our experience shows that your odds of success are higher using our system.

Use the Terms to Sweeten the Project

> ## Jerry
> Years ago, a mentor told me, "It's never about the price; it's always about the terms." Now this doesn't mean that you should go crazy and offer three times the price on a deal because price doesn't matter. It means if you have a plan for this property and it makes cash flow or has equity already built in, then you can start playing with the terms to make the deal work for both parties. Maybe you offer more and the owner carries with a low interest for a specified time. The lesson is look at every deal from multiple different angles, because the terms could turn a C+ deal into an A+ deal.

There are circumstances where you can make a property better by tweaking the terms. We have already talked about how the profit can nearly be doubled by paying lenders 8% to 12% rather than sharing 50% of the profits with investors who fund the projects with no interest at all. This is how you should be looking at the terms of your projects.

If you do the right work, you will have options. If you only have one lender or one investor willing to partner with you, you have no options and only one set of terms. If you have a dozen willing partners and investors, then you can analyze each property against the terms you get from each of your investors until you find the option that nets you the most money. Remember, this is where your ability to analyze opportunities will be the deciding factor. Investors don't like risk!

Purchasing a property with owner financing is one of the few circumstances where you can use the terms to make the actual deal itself.

> ## Terence
> I'm looking at a multi-family property right now where the owner wants 40% down and will finance the rest at 6% interest. It's a $400,000 property that needs a lot of work, so there is no way I would put any of my own money down. I plan to offer close to full price, but

with the owner carrying the entire $400,000 at 6% with his note being a second mortgage behind a $100,000 private first mortgage for the rehab.

If he doesn't take that, I have 10 more adjustments I can make until it might work for him. I'll start at 6% to 7% interest for his note, so in each round of negotiating, I can increase it by 1%. I can also increase the private first by $25,000 at a time, but maybe reduce my offer price as I do it. So if the seller really wants some cash in hand now, maybe he will get $50,000 up front from my private lender, who will now be financing $150,000, but now the owner will only be carrying $350,000 or $325,000.

However it works, my goal on this project is just to own it. Once I own it and can do the rehab, I think I can get the gross rents to a little over $5,000. But the property includes a few acres of extra commercial land, which I think will take me a year to split off, and then I can sell it for close to $300,000. At that point, I can refinance the units at a 5.5% interest rate on an approximately $200,000 mortgage and net over $2,000 per month forever. This is what the terms can do for you.

It's the same on a small scale with single-family properties. I have recently had projects where the sellers wanted super fast closes and were willing to drop their price accordingly. Boom, done.

I just did a project where the sellers needed someone to buy their house and let them stay on for 10 days after close and were willing to take a $20,000 discount to get that, thank you sir, may I have another..

And I have bought lots of houses through online auctions where you must be able to deal with their ridiculous terms and timelines. They refuse to turn on utilities for inspections, and inspection periods are only five to seven days or non-existent. There are no contingencies, so your deposit of $2,000 to $6,000 is at risk from day one if you bail. There are very few buyers who will agree to these terms, which means that few people bid on these properties. And that means I can buy them for $30,000 to $40,000 less than they would sell for if they were being sold with traditional escrows. Yes, that was easy.

More often it's the sellers' terms that make the opportunities for you.

Be Creative

The best part about real estate is that it allows you to get creative. We like doing the things others say can't be done. Now, this isn't in regards to ripping off seniors or doing weird contracts such as net deals, double escrows, and all the things that seem like they could be against the law and are against the law in most states. Please be aware of those. But don't take your creative hat off.

Banks are not the creative types, for the most part. That is unless you find the right banker and the right bank. Sometimes, small banks in local areas will get creative with you.

Jerry

A vice president at one of the largest banks in the western United States got creative with me when I was a new investor. At the time, I had five properties, and all of them had a little positive cash flow. Because the vice president was able to change my loans that were at around 10% down to around 6%, my cash flow went up substantially on each of those properties. It replaced my old income as a producer in the entertainment industry, and almost overnight I was retired. I haven't worked for anyone since!

The beautiful thing is that when you get creative and stay positive by asking different people the same questions, someone might say yes. So stay positive! Remember, what could you accomplish if you could not fail? And when one door closes, another opens. It is just how it works. We wouldn't have Harry Potter if J.K. Rowling stopped writing because people said no one would read her books.

Private money is the best thing in the entire real estate world. *Private money is much more conservative than the banks, but it is more creative.* Private lenders know the power of leverage. They don't want to leave their money in a bank at 1% if they can lend it to you at 6%,

8%, 10%, 12%, or 15%. They will find a way to lend it as long as the offer makes sense. Make it a part of your being that you don't bring your investors opportunities that don't make sense. If it makes sense, you will have no problem getting the money.

Don't Fall Victim to Your Own Terms

A final word of caution: We did a project about 10 years ago and thought we were real estate geniuses when the seller agreed to provide seller financing at 6% with no due on sale clause, no prepayments, etc. We resold the property as the market crashed without paying off the existing financing, and we got the new buyer to pay 7% interest, which gave us the 'spread' between that rate and the 6% we were paying. Long story short, the property made a theoretical $100 extra per month for nearly a decade with no money invested, but the time, effort, and costs associated were much more, so it was a complete waste of time and energy. This is a case where we got tricked by our own terms. Had that junky house and triplex just been offered without any creative terms, we would never have been interested, never would have wasted the time, and never would have bought it. Be smart and use terms for your benefit. You definitely don't want to become a victim of your own terms.

We have done numerous contracts that required special terms. If you are dealing with a multi-family property, and the owners either own it outright or have a small loan on it, or even a single-family home, then just open the book of terms and let them participate. Suggest that they can carry the loan, or if they want to sell but can't do so for a year, do a lease with an option to purchase later. Or if they have a business in the building, you can do a lease back. There is no end to the creative ways to buy real estate.

Jerry

I recently had a property in Costa Rica, and I gave the buyers great terms. If I had insisted on selling the property for $200,000 cash, it would have been difficult for me to sell it at the time. Instead, I offered the property with half down, and I agreed to carry the other half for three to five years. Now I get my money back out of the property, but I also get multiple streams of income from it by having $100,000 working for me at 8%, giving me cash flow. Eventually, I will have more than the full-price offer I was looking for from the beginning, and an extra $21,000 to $35,000 as monthly cash flow. Sweet right? Well the buyers ended up not going for it and passed. I could have been bummed but I happen to be in an up market right now. In the time that we were working on the terms that I would have been happy with and would have brought me more money I ended up selling the property for $245,000. In 3 months I made $45,000 extra. Remember delays aren't always denials.

If you own a piece of property outright, you get to play with the terms however you like. Think, "If I buy this property, how can I make the best offer possible for the seller?" If you think of it from the seller's point of view, then you can come up with fun terms. Real estate agents who just want their listings to sell won't think about this, so get your creative hat on and you will make five times more than you did last year.

CHAPTER 7

THE ESCROW PART I

Terence

I recently made an offer on a small commercial property that I thought had great potential. One of my investor friends had been interested in the property in 2006 for a sales price of $625,000. Ten years later, the owner had chased the market down for years, let two of the buildings fall into disrepair and become vacant, and accepted my low offer of $160,000. I was very pleased with myself and started making grand plans for the miraculous transformation I was going to make in my new corner of downtown.

The more I planned and envisioned what it could be, the higher the price of the renovations climbed. I went through the property with my contractor, talked with the building department, and bragged about the offer to a few of my close colleagues. Everyone thought it was a great project.

Then I visited the property with one of my lenders. It didn't help that during our midday visit, no less than three homeless people visited the property, but my lender just saw too many question marks. He and his wife had financed countless properties for me, sometimes sight unseen. They had financed a mobile home with convicts living in it, a house that had been run as a dog grooming business, houses in flood plains, and houses with every scrap of wire and plumbing torn out of them, but they didn't want to touch this one. I had gotten myself excited about the project, and I still thought it could be a winner, but our goal is to make this business as much about sure things as possible, so I trusted their instincts and canceled my escrow.

Reflect on the Offer and Do Your Homework

This is the whole point of escrow. It's a time to reflect on the offer, a time to gather the opinions of trusted partners and colleagues, and a time to fine-tune that off-the-cuff estimate from your contractor. Many investors get properties in escrow and assume everything is going to work out. Sometimes it can even be an issue of pride or stubbornness, of not wanting to admit that they were wrong. Would you rather be wrong or lose $20,000? Or end up in litigation? Or figure out too late that the property you bought is about to be red-tagged and is a total teardown? We are already buying problem properties, but there is always something that can go even more wrong than you initially imagined. This is what escrow should be used for.

Jerry

One time when I moved into a new market, I identified many properties that were superb opportunities, and I had seven escrows open. Then one day, my agent said something that was not only unethical, it also made me question every detail and bit of information that he was giving me which didn't make me feel safe going forward with the escrows.

Now, why did I do that? Because if you get that feeling in escrow, chances are you are right. For me, it was better to go back and start from scratch. I have never worked with that agent again.

You must trust your instincts when you are in escrow. Don't spend the money for all your inspections on the first day of escrow, especially if you're a new investor. If you have a decent inspection period, ideally 14 to 21 days, let the escrows run their course a little bit. Get the preliminary title report and make sure there are no title issues before you start spending money. Depending on the property, you might then start with your termite inspection, which shouldn't run more than $100. If that looks good, proceed to a whole house inspection. If that looks fine, then move on to the more expensive inspections, like the well or septic, which can run $400 to $600. If the termite inspection or home inspection exposes $15,000 in unanticipated problems, either cancel or negotiate a credit or price reduction. If you can't get a reduction and the numbers don't work with the new costs, now is the time to cancel, before you've invested another $600 to $1,000 on inspections for a property you're never going to buy.

Terence

One of my home inspectors typically charges $225 for inspections for my clients. He goes through dozens if not hundreds of components and gives them a fancy 30-page report. I don't need a fancy report, and I don't need to have every doorknob, cabinet door, and window checked. Those things are all probably getting demolished anyway. I just need to know if there is a major issue that I'm missing. I want to know how the crawlspace and attic look. For an inspection with no written report, my home inspector charges me $100. It's well worth it to get an extra set of eyes on the property. For me, it's worth $100 just to save me from crawling under a house or having to go into an attic or out onto a roof.

Use the escrow period to do as much homework and planning as you can. It will make your resale escrow sail through. At the very least, walk the property and take notes with your contractor, hire a pest inspector to identify any termite or pest work, and hire a home inspector.

If there is an old air conditioner, make sure it's serviced and inspected. And if there is a well or septic tank, pay the money to have it inspected. These are the big-ticket items that you don't want to be wrong about. Some counties have been in a drought for the past few years with aquifers drying up in some of the outlying areas. If your well runs dry and there simply is no water, your house has just about become worthless. If you could have paid $300 to find out that the well was only producing a quarter of a gallon a minute and was running out in less than an hour, that would have been the best $300 you ever spent. The same holds true with septic tanks.

Terence

I once had a house with a septic that was red tagged by the environmental health department. My plumber assured me that it was at most a $3,000 fix, but neither he nor I spoke directly with the inspector who had red tagged the system. I did my $3,000 fix and found out deep into my resale escrow that the inspector was insisting on a whole new engineered system. It added two months to my escrow and more than $10,000 in extra costs, not including my interest, taxes, insurance, and utilities for the extra two months. A 10-minute visit to the county would at least have given me the chance to renegotiate with the sellers, and it would have saved me the extra two months since I could have planned that work from the beginning.

Many investors resist being proactive with these items because they think they will get buyers who either don't notice the problems or want the house so badly that they won't ask. This might happen in super-hot markets, but in most normal markets, the buyers or their agents will expect these things to be done. And now, in many markets, if the buyers are getting any type of government-insured loan, the appraiser may ask that these things will be done. So you might as well do them with your contractor on the front end. This will also save weeks of waiting for vendors to come back out to make small repairs during your escrow, which saves you money and gets you on to the next project that much more quickly.

Terence

I just sold a small multi-family property to a cash buyer, and the escrow closed in just two weeks. The only reason this deal could go together so quickly was that I already had pest inspections and home inspections on every unit available to that buyer before they even made their offer. I didn't have to wait two weeks to get an inspector out and then another week for the buyer to review the reports and risk that they would be surprised by what they found. They already knew what they were getting into on the front end. The more you can engineer this, the better.

Consult the Local Building Department

Many investors try to avoid their local building departments or don't want to bring unwanted attention to their projects. But if there is anything questionable, it's better to risk a full inspection than to rush into a project uninformed and find out that it's already on the building department's radar.

Terence

An investment group that I worked for bought a beautiful country house that was bank-owned. It was a nice two-story house in decent condition with a recently built pool and a large barn. There were no issues recorded on title, the renovation went smoothly, and I got the property in escrow with a strong buyer who was anxious to close.

Unfortunately, about two weeks before our resale escrow was scheduled to close, the buyers stopped by the building department to ask about adding another shop building. To their surprise, they were told that both the pool and the barn had been tagged with notices of non-compliance, and the barn might have to be torn down! The title officer confirmed that a notice of non-compliance was now showing in the preliminary title report. The buyer didn't have time to wait for us to solve the problem and canceled. I spent the next four months working with two different contractors before we finally got an agricultural exemption on the barn and a final permit on the pool.

So why didn't the non-compliance show up when my clients bought it? The county had cited the property more than three years earlier with the former owners who had built the pool but never recorded the notice of non-compliance. The house was foreclosed and owned by the bank for almost a year, and they still didn't record it. They finally recorded the non-compliance about a week after my clients had purchased the home. It cost my clients thousands of dollars and could have been avoided with a five-minute visit to the county building department.

Always assume the worst and make yourself do the work to prove yourself wrong. Remember it is great to be an optimist to get the offer going, but you must become a pessimist during your escrow period. Use the escrow period to save yourself unwanted expense, stress, and headaches.

Plan and Get Bids

This period should also be a time for planning your project and getting bids from your contractor or subcontractors. The more you poke around with a professional, the more at ease you will feel because you are lowering the risk of surprises popping up. Once you become certain that you are buying the property, it can also be a good time to get a running start at having plans drawn if you are doing an extensive remodel. If you are paying 10% to 12% interest, you can save a lot of money by using this free no-interest period to get things moving.

Visit the Property

If the house is vacant, visit the property every week. If a pipe breaks or there is a leak in the ceiling, you can let the owner, asset manager, or agent know and get this fixed at their cost before it causes more damage to the home.

On bank-owned properties and short sales, no one else is going to care about the condition of the home or what is happening to it while you're in escrow, so you had better keep an eye on things. Just your regular visits and presence at the property might keep away vandals, local teenagers, and squatters. If someone does break in and kicks holes in all the walls and rips out all the wiring, it is better to find out before escrow closes while you still have a chance to either cancel if the damage is significant, or negotiate a favorable credit or repair from the seller.

Don't be complacent; visit the property at least weekly. You will see something new and get different ideas for your renovation every time you visit the house, so the more time you spend there, the better. Your initial plan may not always be your best or most profitable plan. Your greatest revelations about how to complete a remodel or how to save money will usually come about the third or fourth time you visit a property.

Identify Your Best Partners and Negotiate Price

This escrow period is also your time to shop your lenders or partners and make sure you're using the best one for this specific project.

After you have completed your inspections, you have a window to make a last-ditch effort for a better price or a repair credit. There is a difference between negotiating price or credits during the initial offer and the escrow period. When the sellers have just put their property on the market, and they are receiving multiple offers, they are not very likely to take an extra $5,000 off their price or kick in for a new HVAC unit. But if you are just a few days from closing, and you hit them with your request, they are more likely to do it since they are already spending their proceeds in their head, if not already on their credit cards. So after you have used escrow to complete all of your inspections and review any big-ticket items, go back and ask for the credit. This is going to be much more successful than just trying to low-ball every offer so much that you never get one accepted.

A final note for clarity: your initial offer must be good enough to make the project work for you, but that extra credit or discount during escrow is the icing on the cake and another strategy that will ensure the longevity of your business.

Terence

I know some aggressive investors who try to negotiate price or credits on every escrow just as a matter of practice. This has not been my approach since there are only about 12 or 15 good REO and short sale agents in my market. If I started hammering them on every escrow with no valid cause, they would be a lot less receptive to my next offer. I think I have made a lot of money by making legitimate offers, rarely canceling, and almost never coming back to the table to ask for unwarranted repairs or credits. If that agent gets three offers, I have a great chance of beating out the competition because I have been reliable and honest, and I have always closed on time.

Choose an Escrow Officer You Enjoy Working with

One of the most important components of the escrow period is the escrow officer himself. It is no fun doing the types of escrows we do with stodgy, unhelpful old warhorse escrow officers. We are doing a lot of properties, so we should get a little bit of extra attention and help from our escrow and title people. It's easier by far to handle an escrow file financed by a private lender than it is to deal with banks and mortgage brokers. But many escrow officers are so much in the box that they just don't get it, or they make everything more complicated than it has to be.

Make sure you are dealing with people who understand what you are trying to do and try to pick some you enjoy communicating with. Hopefully, your escrow officers will share your sense of humor, or at least your style of communicating. You must be able to communicate what you need without feeling like you're putting them out. Your personalities should go together well for it to be a successful match. There is no point in doing all this if you don't enjoy the people you are working with.

Jerry

I love the escrow officer I use in Utah. She is somebody who I like to hang out with, and on top of it, she is an incredibly useful resource. Whenever I am in town, I go see her. She lets me in on what is going on in the market because she knows that much better than I do. I only get to see a tiny portion of what is going on, but she gets to see 150 closed contracts a month in her office. She tells me what she thinks, which way the market is going, what is closing, and where real estate is selling. She also lets me know whether there are a lot of credits being given at the moment, if there are offers that are going over asking, and lots of other great insights from the contracts she sees crossing her desk.

Terence

I have tried many escrow officers, and with some, every change I wanted to make or everything I wanted to do felt like pushing a rock uphill and was met with resistance. It took me lots of trial and error to find the right people, and in my area, there are only three title and escrow companies. In a larger market, it could take a long time to find the right people, but make sure to keep looking until you find your perfect match. Having the right escrow officer on your team will make your business run much more smoothly.

This is another area where it helps to get to know other flippers and investors. It's very easy to ask them who they are using, and those escrow officers will be well-versed in doing your kind of transaction. And it's not a problem for escrow officers or title officers to have 10 or 50 extra contracts. That's great for their company. It doesn't hurt other investors to share the people they work with either because they might get better service for referring your business.

Keep in mind that escrow can be a very frustrating time, depending on who you use as a lender, or if you negotiate with a hostile seller or bank. When your escrow officers present you with what you think are ridiculous requests, remember that these are not coming from the escrow officers; they are just the messengers. Always cut them a little bit of slack because they are dealing with all parties.

Jerry

When you are dealing with your one or two escrow officers, you are not only dealing with them but also with a larger company. Their business has conference rooms, receptionists, copy machines, and maybe even decent coffee. If I have an escrow that is closing, and I want to talk to another potential client, I'll have my meeting at the escrow office. I have never worked with a title and escrow company that has not let me use a conference room or office for business meetings.

Even though people are getting better about having their meetings at Starbucks or a coffee shop, if you want to have a professional meeting and impress in a professional environment, call your escrow officers and ask if you may use their signing room at whatever time you need.

Terence

A very important side-note when buying homes through online auctions: Do not let the auction company use their in-house title and escrow servicers. They will pitch it as, "Hey, we'll get you a discounted rate, and we'll cover our half of the costs if you go with our escrow company." However, using their company is very difficult and tedious because they run many of those escrows from overseas – yes, overseas – so you don't know the people, and they can be challenging to communicate with. It's very bureaucratic and time-consuming.

I always choose to use my local people. The auction company will push back and try to tell you it's going to double your escrow costs. They put the burden on you and say, "Then you have to pay 100% of the fees." I find that even if it does end up costing $600 or $800 more, it's well worth it to have your regular people working on your offer. It will save you time, and with a binder credit for your resale, it won't cost you much more money, if any at all.

My main escrow officers and their assistants know me and my methods very well. They anticipate problems and usually solve them for me before I even hear about them. They know that I always want a binder to save money on the resale escrow, they remind me to order insurance or inspections, and they will push for special recordings even if we have missed the daily cut-off by 10 minutes. They know it's going to cost me another day of high interest, so they make sure I don't get stuck with an escrow carrying over a long weekend if they can help it. They are part of the team. They want me to succeed because they know that means more success and more business for all of us.

THE REHAB

"It was the best of times, it was the worst of times." It sounds like Charles Dickens was talking about the rehab process. He went on to say, "It was the spring of hope, it was the winter of despair." And again, it sounds like many of our rehabs. But they don't have to be this way with the right contractor, the right plan, and the right expectations.

Find the Right Contractor

Let's start with the contractor. It is paramount to get a contractor you jive with.

> ### Jerry
> At the beginning of my investment career, I happened to work with a few contractors who were super-high energy. I realized that type of energy was not good for me to work with because we found ourselves butting heads all the time. I found that if I used a mellower and less frenetic contractor, we could work through challenges that would pop up and handle those much better and with more level heads.

> ### Terence
> If you work with the right people, the relationships will come effortlessly, and some will even become friendships. If you work with people who aren't a good match for you, communication will be a struggle. I have worked with some very skilled and organized contractors who have done great work, but if we have completed a project and I'm still struggling to communicate with them, it's too exhausting. They must match my personality.

> I had one excellent contractor who constantly hounded me about money. He would complete a task and would want me to pay him before the sun went down that day. I found myself running to my lenders to get draws and taking time out of my days to accommodate his rigid pay schedule. It was too stressful, so I found a contractor who has built his whole business around doing work for banks and asset management companies. They always take 30 to 60 days to pay him for anything, so he loves that I pay steady draws throughout the project. We also communicate very openly and honestly, so if he tells me he is getting spread thin, I'll pay a draw early. Conversely, if one of my lenders happens to be traveling, which as wealthy retirees, they are likely to do, he doesn't mind if he has to carry me on a project for an extra few weeks. This way of working might be too casual for you, but this is what works for me and makes my life stress-free.

Finding the right contractor is a balancing act. You're trying to find someone who is experienced enough and reputable enough to be busy, but not so busy that they aren't responsive to your calls or fully engaged in your projects. They need to be organized enough and have a large enough organization to delegate and leverage labor, but not so big that they don't know your projects intimately or so bloated that they can't keep tight cost controls. They must be able to provide high-end work for a low-to-medium price. They must be solvent enough to front some of their material, subcontractor, and labor costs, but not so flush with cash that they are not hungry for your next project.

This delicate balance can be very hard to find, so unfortunately, you may slip off the razor's edge a few times before you find your perfect contractor. And even after you find him or her, they can sometimes get too busy later, raise their prices, lose their best workers, get their license suspended, move on to custom home building, relocate, or simply get burned out on flips.

Terence

I have lost contractors to all those circumstances. I have also had to survive a lot of projects with the wrong contractors and could fill an entire book with horror stories.

One contractor used the wrong fitting on a toilet valve, and the tiny leak almost flooded the entire house. Another went over our 30-day construction schedule by six months! I got an initial estimate for a major project at $130,000, and by the time we worked through all the details, it climbed to over $220,000. One contractor did a beautiful job on a rehab, everything in the house looked great, and I paid the final bill. The house went into escrow a month or two later, and during the buyer's inspections, they discovered that not a single drain line had been connected under the house, so when the inspector turned on all the valves, water gushed into the crawlspace! When I called the contractor, he seemed annoyed with me and asked, "Why didn't you tell me it went into escrow? I would have gotten all those lines finished." Wow.

I have seen crooked walls, interior paint on exterior walls, stucco fights between rival plastering crews, padded time cards, and bogus overruns. I have seen people substitute used appliances and HVAC equipment while billing for new, screw toilet paper holders directly into brand new cabinet faces as handles (how creative!), and try to use salvaged wet bars from a demolished hotel for bathroom vanities (it's weird but true!). Maybe I could fill two books. Even your favorite contractors will make strange decisions, leave things unfinished, or rely on incompetent help.

The first step to mitigating some of these nightmares is research. With any potential employee or certainly any contractor, the easiest way to avoid problems is to ask for references. It seems like few people do anymore. Then oddly enough, even if they do ask for references, they never call them.

When you do call the references, you must listen closely. Some angry past clients will have no problem venting about the terrible job the contractor did on their kitchen remodel, but a lot of people feel bad or don't want any drama, so they speak in code or hope that you will read between the lines. If they answer your questions with clipped monosyllabic answers and no embellishment, they probably weren't that thrilled with the finished project. But if they rave and go into lots of detail about every feature of their new master bathroom, you know it was probably a job done right.

Here are four questions you can ask a reference. This way, you can stay on track, not waste their time, and move toward hiring the contractor or move to the next one.

1. Did they go over budget?
2. Did they complete the project on time?
3. Did they deliver a quality product?
4. Did they respond quickly to communication? Phone calls, texts, or emails?

Ask for pictures of the contractors' latest projects and look closely at them. Ask to visit a current project and see how they run their job sites, how they interact with their workers or subcontractors. Find out how long they have been on the job, and see how much progress they have made in that time.

Understand the Process

Contractors will often underestimate the time a project will take. Again, even if our good contractors tell us four weeks for a rehab, we know it will be five to six, and that is if we stay on them. If we just sit back and don't push, it can easily turn into eight or even 10 weeks.

Terence

To prevent running behind schedule, you first must understand how it happens. I would say I don't want to get too technical, but I want to get so technical with this that you understand it better than your contractor does. It comes down to preparation and planning.

I will use the example of a relatively basic project I'm working on right now. It's a small house, only 15 years old, on a slab foundation, on a city lot with an attached garage. Even though the carpets were stained with oil (even the carpet in the closets), the house itself was not intentionally abused or damaged. I didn't have to move any walls, and I wasn't even putting in new cabinets, just new Formica countertops, which I have only done on a few occasions. I almost always use granite.

Here is my list of repairs in their proper chronological sequence:
- Remove carpet, baseboard, old appliances, and fixtures
- Patch drywall
- Prepare for paint
- Install tile in bathrooms
- Install baseboard in bedrooms
- Paint
- Install countertops
- Install fixtures
- Landscape installation and sprinkler repair ongoing
- Repair fence
- Install kitchen appliances
- Replace garbage disposal that turned out to be defective
- Touch up paint
- Paint garage floor
- Heavy cleaning and window washing
- Pressure wash driveways
- Light staging

My contractor thought he could get this project done in just over two weeks. Instead, it took exactly one month. I never expected it to be two weeks, especially with spring break right in the middle of the project.

As far as my projects go, this one was very easy. I left many components in place like bathroom vanities, some plumbing fixtures, and all the doors. Usually, there are at least a few broken doors, so I typically replace them all to modernize the property, but these were all perfect.

Even as easy as this project was, there were still six distinct subcontractors to negotiate with. On a big project where everything is subbed out, there could be 12 to 15. For every different subcontractor, there is a chance for a new delay. If the painter shows up and the demo or drywall isn't done, he will put another job ahead of this one. So it might not be a one-day delay; it could be up to a week delay if he doesn't feel it's ready. My general contractor supplies most of the materials, so if the tile-setter shows up and the tile or grout isn't on site, he might pull off and squeeze in another quick project until everything is ready. That could be a few days. If the countertops aren't installed on time, the plumber can't install the sink, garbage disposal, and dishwasher. If the guys are still working on the house, the cleaner doesn't want to get started because they are constantly making new messes, so she will pull off and wait an extra day.

So even on a simple project, there can be five to six delays of one to five days each. It can add up to a month of wasted time, which is a month of wasted interest, utility cost, insurance cost, and maintenance costs.

You can avoid a lot of these delays simply by having the right contractor. If he is giving his subs a lot of work, or if he has his own salaried crew that can perform multiple trades, they won't risk delaying his job and will keep any delays minimal.

Make a Written Plan

You can also reduce delays by sitting down with your contractor and creating a written plan. Even if you are the one to write everything out while you discuss the list of tasks, just give him a copy at the end of the meeting or email a draft to him with your time estimates or schedule and get him to confirm the schedule.

When you visit the job site, bring a new copy of the schedule with you and confirm where you are in the process. It won't take much of this for the contractor to understand that you expect him to be accountable to the schedule. It's not theoretical; it's a living document that can even be tacked up at the job site so that the other subcontractors can see it.

If you have good rapport with your contractor, creating a contract won't be uncomfortable. And *you must have a contract*. If you don't, you might as well just go outside with $100 bills and start your barbecue with them because that is how much money you will lose. Even if your contractor is a family member, you still need a contract. With a good contract, you can expect to have a decent friend and a lot of surprises along the way. With a great contract, you are still going to have surprises, but you will have a nice rehab with less stress.

Terence

I have made extensive, 10-page long contracts where every detail and component of the job was itemized. In fact, I had one contract from an insurance-oriented contractor that was 40 pages. Every roll of tape, every pair of rubber gloves, and every trash bag was itemized on the estimate. If you are very detail-oriented, knowing all those things might give you a level of comfort, but for me, that kind of structure and micromanagement is too much. I feel like if someone spent 15 hours crafting the estimate, I'm going to spend too much money with that contractor. Everything is a little too much in their favor.

> The other side of the coin is being too casual and loose. With a lot of my contractors, it's a struggle to get any written estimate or contract, or they may give me a very generic form without a lot of detail. That too can be a little scary because things will be missed.
>
> I like to put my expectations in writing, so that is commonly what we do. That written plan becomes their actual estimate. Then we know we are on the same page with what things are getting covered.

When you are starting out, and you don't know the people you will be working with, everything must be in writing, and everything must be signed. After you have done 10 or 15 projects over a span of years with the same contractors, you will get to a comfortable spot with them. But that isn't to say there couldn't be problems or litigation. Something can always happen. It's in your best interest to have a clear plan in writing with the contractors.

A typical rehab estimate is about two to three pages of basic rehab like the one we described earlier in the chapter, and it should have a decent amount of clarity. On a one-page contract, which is what most contractors will give you for their estimate, there probably won't be more than eight to 12 line items.

Penalties

Terence

I have never written penalties into contracts, but some of my colleagues do. If you have done your homework, have the right contractor, and can visit the site frequently, penalties might not be necessary. If you suspect you have the wrong contractor, but for some crazy reason you are going ahead with him anyway, then I would recommend having the strongest possible terms in your contract, including late penalties. And if you are not working face to face with the contractors, and you don't have a long-term relationship with them, I recommend using the more strongly worded contracts.

Jerry

You also need to learn what is legal and what is not legal in your area. I do rehabs in different states and even different countries. I discovered that if I have a contract in English for a job in Costa Rica, it's worthless because it must be in Spanish to be upheld in court in Costa Rica. This was good for me to know because I used a contract with my builder that I use all the time. I call it the carrot and stick. The carrot is a huge bonus if the contractors finish early. For example, if they finish a month early on a six-month contract, the bonus could be an extra $5,000. If they are moderately early, they receive a smaller bonus. For example, if they finish two weeks early, they get $1,000 extra. I'm happy to pay bonuses, but of all the rehabs I have done, I have never had to give a carrot. If they finish on time, there is no bonus at all. Every single day after the time the contractors said the project would be finished, it costs, for example, $100. That is the stick. It depends on your market and your rehab, but this is the penalty I use.

When I did a new building in Costa Rica, I had the contractor sign the contract with that exact system of a giant golden carrot, a small carrot, no carrot, and then a penalty. He chose to take another gig when the house was 96% done. He took most of his crew from my house, and he let it go for some months before finishing it. I was on vacation at the time, and when I came back, he hadn't finished it. After he did finish it, and he was looking for his last payment, we sat down, and I said, "You aren't going to get $15,000 of your final payment because you decided to take another job and didn't complete the project on time."

If they sign it, they know it. Remind them of it because it makes it very clear, and clarity is power.

If your contractor likes your contract, he can do the same thing with his subcontractors.

When you create the contract, the contractor sets the timeline. If he tells you that it's going to be four weeks, and it ends up being eight weeks, there is going to be a huge problem. So make sure he gives you a realistic timeline. Say, "You are writing the contract, so if you think it's going to be eight weeks, write eight weeks. If you think it's going to be 10 weeks, write 10 weeks; don't write four weeks because at the end of the day it is going to be wasting my time and your money." Then the contractor will know that you are going to be happy with their work when they finish on time or early.

Visit Your Projects

If you are working with a new contractor, you should visit the job site every day. That doesn't mean stay there all day and get in their way or micromanage their every move. It means stop in for 15 minutes in the morning after they have been at it for a while to see how things are going to make sure everyone is showing up and to correct any mistakes before it's too late. Bring a clipboard and write as you go through the site. Take out your camera and snap a few pics. This will be a log, and the workers will probably work better because they know they are being monitored and recorded.

Jerry
When I built my first home in Costa Rica, I arrived one day before they started digging all of the holes to pour the cement for their columns, and they had the house 45 degrees the wrong way!

Terence
I just stopped at one of my projects where we were completely remodeling the kitchen, and they had framed a wall for a kitchen peninsula that was the same height as the lower cabinets. I wanted a raised breakfast bar to give some separation and make a more dramatic backsplash with outlets for appliances. The framer and electrician were both on site, and it was a 20-minute fix. If I had not

come out until a week later, it would have been a $500 fix for new drywall, framing, and moving electrical, and it could even have messed up the granite order. You must visit your projects.

I also meet with my contractors a lot off site. If they have questions or samples they want me to see, I'll meet them at The Home Depot or, you guessed it, I'll meet them for lunch. Everybody loves to go to lunch. Plus in the 45 minutes we sit there, we will each think of 10 more things we had questions about.

Remember that opportunities also come from lunches. I just went to lunch with my lead contractor and was kicking myself, thinking I might be eating out too much, spending too much money. But suddenly my contractor started telling me about an opportunity he had come across that might work for me. I texted the seller while we ate, set an appointment to see the house 30 minutes later, and wrote a contract on the house 90 minutes after that, just barely beating out one of my competitors. It's a fantastic project that might make me $50,000 and will give my contractor another $50,000 rehab project. Our lunch at Famous Dave's only cost $35! That's a pretty good return.

When you start assuming that the contractors know what they are doing, you will start having problems. You must make yourself the expert. The mistakes we described are commonplace. It's not unusual for us to visit a home and an appraiser tapes out at 2,132 square feet while the plan shows slightly smaller square footage because whoever originally laid out the footings missed the measurement by one to two feet. People all along the way—the building inspectors, the general contractor, the concrete contractor, and everybody else—kept making the same mistake.

We are laymen, yet we have caught monumental mistakes both with new construction and renovation projects—mistakes we would have thought any novice tradesperson would notice, yet there can be six people on a job site, and no one sees it. Be present, be trained, be alert to what is going on, and don't assume that they know better than you do. No one cares more about your money than you.

Communicate

Communication is the key. The written plan is the first step in communicating your expectations with your contractor. If he has five other projects, he might forget when he promised to have yours done. That is why the written plan is so important.

Be the squeaky wheel. If they finish early, reward them. It doesn't always have to be huge money; it can be pizza on site or a wrap party. Include everyone from the contractor to the escrow people.

When you walk through the project, give the contractor as much detail as you can about your preferences. This goes for types of materials, paint colors, style and color of appliances and fixtures, door style, hardware, carpet colors and style, plants or landscape materials, types of granite or Formica, and even drywall and stucco troweling. He will love you if you pick all the paint colors, fixtures, and hardware. Not only does it save him time, but it also avoids potential cost overages by doing the same job twice.

Try to remember that your contractor is a builder and organizer, not necessarily a designer. Some are phenomenal trendsetters and visionaries, but most will do better work if you give them direction and show them the style or look you are going for. If you are not great with design and color, find someone who is. Everyone knows someone who loves to shop and decorate.

Terence

I'm pretty good with style and design, but I often bring in my, friends, colleagues, and sometimes even my dad to my projects to get fresh ideas or to get second opinions if I'm trying something new.

One of the greatest communication tools between you and your contractor is a roll of blue painter's tape. This is a universal tool that contractors and new homebuilders use toward the end of a project to denote items that need correction.

Do you see an oversized blob of drywall mud, a crooked electrical outlet, or paint overspray? Stick a piece of blue tape on it. If you try just to walk through and point out the items, odds are the contractor will only remember 40% of them. If you email them, it's impossible to explain the exact location of a spot that didn't get paint, or which fixture has that scratch that you can only see in direct sunlight. Stick blue tape on it. Don't be stingy because once they pack up their tools and move on to the next project, it's always harder to get them to come back for a five-minute fix.

It also makes them accountable and raises the standards. Sometimes they know they made those little mistakes, but if they think you're okay with that level of quality, then that is the level of quality they will deliver. The blue tape shows them that you have high expectations and that you are paying attention. No crooked light switch covers in our houses, good sir!

Pay with Credit Cards

Terence

My favorite general contractor and a few of my favorite subcontractors take credit cards, which I love. If you are starting out, this can be a huge help to your cash flow, but I love that I get hundreds of thousands of points and miles on my credit cards every year. I have used these points to book travel and upgrade airline flights and hotel rooms. It may sound trivial, but a few years ago I used just a fraction of the points I had earned to book a first-class flight to New York and two first-class tickets to London. The retail cost of those two tickets was $16,000. Find a contractor that works for you and you too can travel the world!

The beautiful thing about paying a contractor or subcontractor with credit cards is not just that you get to use the points for those fun things like traveling and vacations with your family. It also gives you an extra 30 days to hold onto your cash for surprises. In addition, it gives you points you can use at The Home Depot, Lowes, and all the different vendors where you buy your rehab materials.

Jerry

Many credit card companies will give you offers if you shop a lot at certain stores. The Home Depot and Lowe's credit cards will give you 10% or 20% off your entire order. If you have good credit and are going into a huge remodel, now might be the time to do this because you could save thousands on your first rehab.

American Express gives me electronic coupons that I don't even have to do anything with at The Home Depot and Lowes, so if I spend money at those stores, they automatically give me 20% off what I have spent.

I did a remodel on a house in Los Angeles, and since I wasn't going to be there, I asked the contractor if he would take credit cards through PayPal because that would be an easy way for me to pay him. He didn't know about PayPal, so I educated him about it. As a result, I got to hold on to my cash, and he just added another way to offer a service to his clients.

Optimism Versus Realism

Your rehabs will drive you crazy if you don't go into them with the proper expectations. Sometimes it takes an optimist to look at a run-down, vandalized, thoroughly destroyed house and think that it could become a habitable, happy home again. At the same time, your expectations must be realistic. You can't expect to buy a massive fixer-upper with a bad roof, bad HVAC, old windows, a dated kitchen and bathrooms, and tons of dry rot and think that you will somehow find a hungry contractor to fix it up for $20,000. A filthy kitchen with broken cabinets and torn linoleum can easily become a sparkling new showplace with custom cabinets, granite, new flooring, and upgraded appliances, but it's going to cost $8,000 to $12,000. So that part is easy, but it isn't realistic to think that you are going to do it for $4,000. It's even more dangerous when the eternal optimist in you starts thinking that you can sell a house for $249,900 on a street with 10 comparable sales at $195,000.

If you have done your homework, and you know your market, your costs, and your neighborhoods, you will avoid some of these false expectations. You must be disciplined, even in your optimism. If you can start building this discipline, mental game, and follow-through right out of the gate, the way will be easy for you.

It's easy to fantasize about the process and envision how your project will be transformed, but it's harder when contractors don't show up, you find $6,000 worth of unexpected dry rot or plumbing problems, and the building inspector red-tags your construction project and adds even more upgrades and costs to your project. This is the part where you must dig deep and push through the barriers. It's easy to stay motivated and focused when you think you are going to make $40,000. It's a lot harder to keep pushing on a project when you start to see that it's going to break even or maybe even cost you money. Again, this is where your discipline must kick in. You must get through every project, whether it's a winner, breakeven, or loser, as quickly and efficiently as possible. Sometimes it's a matter of just stopping the bleeding and getting it gone before there is another month of interest, insurance, and utility bills. Sometimes it's important to get the funds back to your lenders so they can be reloaded for that next project that is the big winner. And sometimes you just need to get rid of the negative energy and stress and clear your desk for other opportunities.

Jerry

The television shows about remodeling and rehabs are reality TV, and having worked in television, I can tell you there is nothing real about reality TV. When you see them do these elaborate whole-home remodels in six weeks, they have done a lot before in their favor, and they have huge crews of 30 or so people. The shows are fun to watch, and they are great for ideas, but they do not present realistic timelines.

Terence

Your expectations may change over time as well. When I first started flipping homes, I was much more aggressive about grinding down the prices of contractors, often used cheaper unlicensed tradespeople or handymen, avoided permits, and shopped with coupons or on Craigslist for a lot of my materials. While I think these can all be valuable skills and an overall good practice, my goal now is to focus my energy on finding better opportunities or getting better prices on my initial purchase. When I make a great offer on the front end, I don't have to push my expectations to the breaking point during rehab and my resale.

I met a broker colleague for lunch recently, and as I often do, I pitched him on my upcoming inventory and asked him for his best estimate on pricing. So often in the past, I would be hoping to get $249,900 on a house and my colleagues would tell me "$225,000 max." During this lunch, I noticed that I have reached a new level of success when every price he gave me was $20,000 higher than my highest target sales price. This told me that I have been buying my properties better than ever.

Strangely enough, I have also been paying a little more for my rehabs. I have gotten into a steady groove with my lead contractor, and on many recent projects, I told him to up the budget so we could spend more time on things like detailing, extra cleaning, landscaping, and overall polish.

> I have reached a level of mastery where I now expect everything to be easy. My contractor knows what I like and how I want things done. The houses are coming out at a list price just under market, so they are selling quickly. And the buyers and their agents know they are getting value, so I'm getting easier escrows, fewer problems with pushing appraisals, and fewer repair requests because I have already done the work on the front end. This is all because my expectations are in synch with what I know to be the reality in my market. I'm not expecting to get a $40,000 rehab for $20,000. I'm not expecting to sell a $225,000 house for $250,000. I'm not expecting an eight-week rehab to get done in three weeks.

The rehab process is going to make or break your bottom line because if it takes longer than you intended, it chews up not only your time to market and the money you are paying on the loan and so on. It also cuts out of what you want to do next—the vacation you wanted to go on or more time with family. Don't let rehabs control you and your life. Make a plan that keeps you in control of your rehabs.

If you haven't educated and trained yourself properly, and you are constantly failing to meet your expectations, it can be very demoralizing. At the same time, if you have diligently built your market knowledge, relationships, and systems, you will constantly exceed your expectations, which makes for a much more fulfilling career and a much happier life in general. And this is what we want for you most of all.

Go to our website www.flippingmainstreet.com for sample Rehab Worksheets.

CHAPTER 9

THE SALE PART I
BEFORE THE AGENT

Terence

It's time to make a confession, "Forgive me, Father, for I have sinned. I have not once, but many times put homes on the market that were not quite ready for sale."

"For your penance, sell 10 more and make sure all of your disclosures and inspections are completed before you list them."

Though I know better by now, I even did this last year. I had a house I thought could be a quick turn. I got anxious to get in and get out, so I cut back on a few renovations that I thought might be unnecessary and that I worried would slow down my project. The house had acoustic popcorn ceilings, which are always well worth scraping and retexturing. It doesn't cost a lot of money, and it immediately makes the house feel 20 or 30 years newer. In this case, I wasn't doing any other drywall work, and I thought I could skip the ceilings, save a few bucks, and get the house on the market a few days sooner. The kitchen cabinets were pretty beat up, but I have done dozens of renovations where I have simply cleaned up and painted the existing cabinets with great success. I took a cursory glance at the cabinets and decided to do that on this one. Between the cabinets and the ceiling, I saved about $3,500 in renovation costs.

Flash forward nine months and the house had gone into escrow on three separate occasions. Two of the buyers backed out claiming lender problems. And one cited the home inspection report. But I knew that in all three cases the truth was that on the second or third visit back to the house, they started noticing the ratty cabinets that were crooked and falling apart despite the best efforts of three carpenters and the old, dated acoustic ceilings. I would have backed out too!

So at the nine-month mark, I grudgingly admitted that I was wrong. I spent $2,500 on new cabinets, did some touch-up paint on the ceilings, and did a minor restaging on the house. It went back into escrow for the fourth time at the highest sales price yet, more than the cost of the cabinets. I initially estimated that the house would make about $30,000 in profit, but because of my poor planning and weak finish on the rehab, it only netted about $10,000, and that was with no interest!

A quick side note on how you should treat your partners and investors: *Protect them.* On this particular project, I gave the entire $10,000 profit to my partners who had funded the project. By the time I had paid the last utility bills, I probably lost $1,000 to $2,000 on this project. Why did I give the $10,000 to my investors/partners you wonder? Because I knew deep down that it was my poor decisions that made the project fail, and I felt I should hold myself accountable. I may be my own boss, but sometimes I have to be a tough boss, even to myself! I have only had one other project perform that poorly, and I did the same thing on that one. However, on that one, only about $5,000 went to the investors, and I took a $4,000 loss. Same bad decisions, same accountability.

Taking the loss myself is strategic. These investors have done 20 properties with me, 18 of which have been huge successes. If they know I will protect them and hold myself accountable and even dig in my own pocket to ensure that they always make a reasonable return, they will partner with me forever. If I lose their money, don't take the blame, and show them that I don't care whether they win or lose, that money will probably migrate to someone else. It is much cheaper and easier to pay them a few extra dollars than it is to find new partners, especially ones with whom I enjoy working. Act with integrity and own your mistakes.

There are also many times when you simply get anxious to put a house on the market too soon. Sometimes when you have waited for months for a project to be completed, and you finally see it become a house again, it's hard to resist the urge to "throw it on the market," but resist you must!

Take a deep breath, get out the blue tape, and go through the house as if you were a buyer; as if you were going to stretch your finances to the limit to buy it and raise your family there. What would your expectations be? Would you pay full price if the windows and screens hadn't been cleaned or there was still a pile of construction debris in the middle of the garage? Would you make a full-price offer if a few light fixtures still hadn't been installed, the yard was still a mess, and the dirty old slider still hadn't been replaced? Of course not, yet people list their houses too early all the time. After 30 or 60 or 90 days of rehab, it is well worth a few extra days to make sure everything is perfect—not only perfect for attracting that buyer who wants to make a full-price or over-asking-price offer, but perfect in the sense that the escrow will feel like it's on autopilot.

Get Comfortable with Multitasking

It's important to know the typical cycle for most investors who flip houses. Imagine Henry Ford's assembly line and one person walking the car through the entire process, fumbling with every door handle and bumper, and putting on every piece. No other cars are built while this one is moving down the line. That is how most rehabbers operate. They acquire one or two houses, get buried in the details of the rehab for two to three months, go on the market early, then get buried in the details of selling them for two to three months. They get overwhelmed, and they work so hard to catch up at every stage that they can only buy one or two houses at a time, and they can't even think about writing offers on new properties until those are gone. Then, and only then, do they acquire one or two more houses.

If one house takes longer than expected, they go over budget, and if one ends up having major issues, they have just spent a year of work to make maybe $30,000 or $40,000. If the market shifts or they were wrong on more than one of the houses, they would make less than their cheapest laborer.

They are smart and super ambitious, but so many times, they are either out of money because they haven't done their work to get other lenders or partners in the lending process, or they think they can't take on another project because they are right in the middle of rehab. Or they wait to buy new houses because they feel they can't with these two houses in escrow. That is why most flippers flip fewer than four houses per year. As a result, they are sitting idle when they should be out buying the next two. Many of our colleagues have missed great opportunities on houses because they were too preoccupied with their current projects and escrows. We have reached a point where we are always looking, and we never say no to a great opportunity.

When you feel like you can't add more houses, you need to train your brain to resist that feeling. The best thing to do is look for another project. One of the greatest ways to force your growth is to acquire that especially good project even if you don't know exactly how you are going to finance it. We don't recommend doing this when you are new, but if you are seasoned, have done many properties, and have multiple lenders, this will force you to branch out and find a new lender or new partner to make the opportunity work. It's also a lot easier to start a new relationship with lenders or partners when you have an exceptionally good project to work on with them.

Also, if you work on escrow paperwork, disclosures, or inspections every day, it's easy to get tunnel vision. It's comfortable to keep doing that same activity. It's the same with rehab. If you are in rehab mode, and you are going to your job sites every day, shopping for tile, talking to your contractors, and so on, it's very easy to stay in that mode.

We want you to become comfortable with multitasking—overseeing construction every day and dealing with escrows, but also looking to find new lender partners and opportunities. You should be doing all those things at all times; otherwise, you will have peaks and valleys. You will sell your two properties and have a bunch of money come in, and then you will be completely idle with no more income for six months. You must start completely over finding a project, getting it in escrow, closing that property, doing your rehab, getting it back on the market, getting it through another escrow, and then getting paid again. You must have projects in each of these stages simultaneously, or it's going to make for inconsistent income and cash flow.

Create a Scalable Business

Rather than focusing on your resources, focus on your resourcefulness. Focusing on your resourcefulness is key, or you are only going to be as good as your resources. For example, if there is a team of one guy working only with his family's money and one slow contractor who is also part of the family network, they are not looking to leverage other contractors because they don't want to pay more or make a new relationship. Then they are not using their resourcefulness. If they realized that instead of doing four or five or six projects a year where they did everything themselves, they could oversee 26 a year because of their expertise, then all of a sudden, they could lift the 800-pound gorilla with one finger. Then it would be a scalable business model.

Once you have a scalable business model, you can get lean in lean times and gigantic when there is a ton of inventory. For that reason, focus not just on your resources but also on your resourcefulness. Remember your *why*. You want to be able to expand not in 10 years, but one year.

So let's figure out how to get your sales on autopilot so you can get right into your next opportunities.

Get Your Contractors on Board

In the last chapter, we talked about picking the right contractors, people you are comfortable communicating with. That is the first step because for this to work, you must be able to make the contractors understand that they can't pull their workers off the job until it is truly done. It is very easy to get contractors to do 98% of a project, but it's insanely difficult to get them to finish the last 2%! It might have to do with psychology; they might be so afraid of not having their next job that they never want the current job to end. It somehow makes them feel like they are busy.

The only way to cure this stalling is not to pay them their final check until the house is 100% completed. Make sure they understand that from the beginning, remind them in the middle, and stay strong at the end when they assure you that the last section of fence will be installed tomorrow morning. Too bad. No check until it's done. If you give them the check, the last section of fence might still be missing two months later, and you will have missed five buyers who thought the backyard felt exposed and unfinished or saw the neighbor's junk pile through the missing fence and decided they didn't want to live there.

Now that you have your contractors on board, you must know what needs to be done.

Put Your Best Foot Forward

With most things in life, you find two teams: optimists and pessimists. Studies have found that, over time, pessimists are more right, but optimists do better. The reason is that optimists always think they are doing better than they are. The fact that you are reading this book right now means you are probably an optimist. Real estate investors, for the most part, are optimists. We always think we are doing better than we are. If you continue with that mindset, you are likely to do better than if you have a pessimistic mindset.

In the sale, however, you must be a realist. Being a realist means that when you go through your property, you must put your optimistic glasses aside, put on your realist glasses, and say, okay, what needs to be done here? If you walk through it and think it seems good enough, then chances are you should fix it. Even if it's not a brand-new home, it's new to the people who come through it. You are not going to fix everything in a 30-year-old house, but you will fix most of it. You wouldn't try to sell a car without vacuuming and washing it, and if there were rips and tears, you would mend those. It's the same thing with a home.

Jerry

I used to have a property manager who never thought anybody would sell an investment property. If he knew there would be tenants, he would put in a horrendous purplish brown carpet. The reason he put this carpet in every rental he managed was that it camouflaged dirt, dog poo, pee, mud, blood, and all that stuff. When he started managing properties for me, I told him I wanted all that ripped out, and I wanted laminate flooring put in. He said that people would destroy it, but I said that if you give somebody something they think is bad, then they are going to treat it badly. If you give them something beautiful, it elevates their opinion of it and themselves.

You want to put your best foot forward. Then people will walk in and feel like the property has been taken care of and they don't have to do that work. When people are buying a new home, or it's new to them, they don't want to have to start off by scraping the ceilings, ripping out the carpet, fixing the disgusting garage that has oil stains all over the floor, or putting in new grass outside. Take away all the reasons someone would say no.

Pay Attention to the Details

The devil is in the details. Spend the money to clean the windows, wash or replace the screens, and get the cleaner back one more time if it has been more than a couple weeks since the last visit. When there is even just a little work being done, houses get dusty. Make sure paint lines are clean and crisp. We can spot the choppy lines of a cheap painter before we get out of the car and so can a good agent or an experienced buyer. Freshen up the yard. Even if you haven't done new landscaping, bring in some fresh mulch or gravel, give lawns or planted areas a sharp edge, and make sure you have someone doing weekly yard maintenance while your property is on the market. Keep the pool clean, and haul the final trash off the property.

Don't be cheap. If you have spent $60,000 on a rehab of a high-end 1970s home, don't leave the existing 30-year-old garage door opener with the missing cover and dangling wires. Complete the job; spend $250 to install a new one to match the integrity of the rest of your project. If you are that worried about spending the final $250, it means that you didn't buy the house right, and you didn't plan your rehab right to begin with. The buyers are going to ask for the new garage door opener anyway, yet they already lowered their offer price by $2,500 because it looked so junky, so now you are paying for the opener ten times instead of once! It's also a lot easier to install the opener when you have people working on site. When you are doing repairs after the rehab, it takes a lot more time, costs more money, and if it's major repairs, you will need to clean the house all over again. Do it right the first time.

Keep visiting your property or have someone who does. Stay on yourself and your team to make sure utilities are on, no pipes are frozen, the yard is maintained, the staging is looking good, and newspapers or advertising circulars are not lying in the driveway. You don't want it to look unattended because then it attracts squatters and vandals.

It's also important to befriend the neighbors. Make sure they all have your phone number so if someone sees a lurker, kids playing in the backyard pool, vandals, or a broken sprinkler, they can call you right away. Or they can feel empowered to intervene because they know the circumstances, feel protective of you, and know the players involved and who should or shouldn't be there. Introduce them to your contractor and subcontractors; you want them to feel like a part of the process. If you can get your highest price, you should explain how that benefits them by raising the value of their home. If you are an agent, and they see how well you market your property, when they go to list their homes, you may be the one they call because they know you know the market—you sold the house next door or right across the street after all.

Avoid Discounting Twice

If the work is not done or inspections are not completed, you will have to discount your property twice to keep your offer together. But if you know the house is perfect and financeable, you are somewhat assured that whatever price you initially negotiate with the buyers is the price they are going to pay. So if you give them a $5,000 discount, that is all you give. If you haven't done the work or planning on the front end, you are even more likely to get an offer that is $5,000 less than the asking price or less, but then when the buyers do their inspections, they find out that the house needs another $5,000 to $10,000 in repairs. If now you must agree to another $5,000 in work during escrow, you have essentially discounted your property twice.

Terence

I recently had this situation come up on a flip I did with one of my more stubborn partners. We hadn't done the work or inspections, and the first buyer we got made a low offer. My partner insisted that I would explain to the other agent that we would take the offer, but there wouldn't be any further credits, no matter what. They agreed, and we opened escrow.

After their inspections, they discovered that the property still required a substantial amount of work, and they asked for all of it to be completed. My partner was furious and wouldn't do any of the work, so the escrow canceled. Then he got even more furious and said, "But they agreed that they wouldn't get any more credits." I explained to him that no one can commit or agree to a price without knowing the full extent of the problems with a house or the cost of fixing them."

If you do everything you can to educate the buyers on the condition of the property up front or if you eliminate as many of these potential costs upfront, you will only have to discount your property once, or maybe you won't have to discount it at all.

Sell the Sizzle, Not the Steak

Jerry

Recently, a home in Los Angeles I had rented out for 10 years was vacated when the renter moved on, so I had to decide whether to keep it or sell it. I decided to sell it, and since the market was hot, I decided to do the bare minimum because I thought all I needed was to have someone with a pulse walk through and they would buy it.

Now, it was built in 1929, so it had a tiny one-car garage. Even though it would have cost me just $10,000 or so to make that one-car garage into a two-car garage, I decided against it. Inevitably, it sat on the market for six months.

Everybody who came through had two reasons for not buying it. One was the noise of the freeway, which is a nice way of saying they didn't want to buy the house. All the homes in that area are close to a freeway. The second objection was the one-car garage ("I can't get my Hummer in it"). For me, even as a seasoned real estate professional, it was another lesson that you must fix things that are functionally obsolete. Make them functional for the time you are living in. These days, a lot of people own SUVs, so garages must be able to handle large cars.

I couldn't fix the garage; I was too far into it. I needed to get the property sold, so I had it staged. Within two weeks, I sold it to an all-cash buyer. I made my money, and it showed me once again that you must put your best foot forward or else it will chew into your time. You can get money back, but you can't ever get your time back. It's imperative to keep that in mind.

That brings us to the question of whether to stage homes. The answer is always to stage them. As an investor, it will get your properties sold more quickly, maybe not for more, but they will get sold faster. Also, now you own all the staging equipment. And if you have a staging company do it, it's an expense you write off.

Terence

For years, I resisted staging my houses. I thought it was too expensive and didn't want to waste the time or effort. But a few years ago, I started using professional stagers for my middle and upper-end projects and noticed a big difference. Again, I didn't necessarily sell the homes for a lot more money, but the homes sold more quickly.

On some projects, staging can also save money. Sometimes, if the kitchen is well staged, you can leave the existing countertops if they are still clean and in good condition. It is the same with the bathroom vanities. So if you save $3,000 on countertops, it's well worth spending $1,200 to $1,500 to stage a house and have it sell faster too.

Even on my lower-end projects, I do at least my own light staging with towels, soap dishes, rugs and bath mats, toilet paper, and knick-knacks. And perhaps the best and most often overlooked staging element that might save you hundreds of dollars? A $6.99 doormat from T.J. Maxx or Ross. Not only does it give a house a welcoming and finished look, but it also keeps the idiots of the world from tracking mud all over your brand-new carpet or wood floors.

So to review: Buy the house well enough that you can afford to make even the minor fixes, clear pest work, repair or replace all major systems, and clean and stage the home. Gather inspections, reports, and all disclosures on the front end before you put the home on the market for a lightning-fast escrow, a stronger negotiating platform, and no surprises or last-minute requests for additional discounts or credits. Make sure to have a plan in place to keep the home clean and the yard tidy throughout the marketing and escrow process.

If you follow this plan on each one of your projects, you will keep yourself from getting entrenched in the minutiae, and you will suddenly have more time to stay focused on finding new money and new opportunities. So not only will you be making an extra $5,000 or more on each project, but instead of struggling to do three to four properties a year, you can now do eight or 10 a year with the same effort—like an assembly line where you have houses at every stage at all times. You might be acquiring houses. You have some houses in escrow. You have some houses that are under rehab, and you have some houses that you are marketing. You should be maintaining this whole process effortlessly if you are using our system properly and following these basic rules. Stick with your plan, and you will more than double your income with the same amount of work!

Now that all these pieces are in place, you are ready to start thinking about the agent.

CHAPTER 10

THE SALE PART II
THE AGENT

Even if you are a licensed Realtor, and you handle the sales of your properties, you still need to read this chapter. And if you are not licensed, and you rely on a Realtor to market and handle the sales of your properties, then you should probably read this chapter twice.

Agents fall into three different categories—the good, the bad, and the inexperienced.

The Good Agents

Good agents are seasoned but not jaded. They keep up with the trends. They know their market. They keep up with technology. They better themselves, and they are pleasant to be around. They understand investors, which is imperative because we are investors. You will never complain about paying a percentage to a good or great agent because you know that you are getting your money's worth and a lot more.

Good agents think outside the box, add value, and don't discount your ideas. In his fantastic book *The Difference*, Scott E. Page describes how diversity trumped expertise in every study they did. This is why having an agent that you can bounce ideas off as well as your contractor will help you create a better product and find a better way to sell properties. This is especially true if you have an unusual property. Not every property is a three-bedroom, two-and-a-half bath with a three-car garage and perfect lawn in a perfect neighborhood. Sometimes you need someone who doesn't just think outside the box, but destroys the box and builds a geodesic dome in its place. Sometimes it takes doing something completely different to get a unique property sold.

Jerry

When I first lived in West Hollywood, I was in my mid-20s, and I was getting ready to rent. I pulled up the paper during a major recession, and there were all these places for rent, but the rent was fairly high. Then there was one ad that said, "Why rent when you can own for the same amount of money?" I called even though I didn't have any money or a long-term job. The agent, Ron, was the outlier. He understood real estate. He understood sales. When I called him, he didn't discount me. He took me out and showed me properties, and I ended up buying my first home. To this day, he is one of the top agents in that market. For over 20 years, he has been reinventing and staying up with the times and doing what it takes to be a great agent. Successful people do what others won't, and the same thing goes for agents. Find allies who are doing things outside the norm.

The Bad Agents

You can smell bad agents a mile away. This is why sitting down with the agents is so important. It will allow you to get a feel for whom you jive with. Bad agents are negative. They are negative about the market, the buyers, the sellers, the houses, and the neighborhoods. If you go to Starbucks, they want to go to the mom-and-pop coffee shop; if you go to the mom-and-pop coffee shop, they say that their coffee is too burned because they have crappy roasters. Their negative attitude spills over the cup into their lives. They don't understand thinking out of the box, and they prefer doing things the same way they always do – poorly. There is no need to say it, but we are going to say it anyway: if this agent is your mom or another family member or even your best friend, do not use them!

The Inexperienced Agents

The third type of agent is the inexperienced. Just because they are inexperienced, it doesn't necessarily mean you shouldn't use them. If they are hungry, positive, and open to understanding more about your business, you might want to keep them around. They might even ask to shadow you to learn more about your business and how they can help. Keep them around because these hungry agents might go from selling zero houses to selling 10 or 20 in their first year. They might have something that will make them a valuable part of your team—if not now, then perhaps later. Identify them.

Just because people don't have any experience, it doesn't mean that they can't be great. Most people who say they have 20 years of experience have one year of experience that they have been doing for 20 years. It's better to find people who are always adding new things to their tool belt so that they can pull it out as trends and cycles change. The inexperienced can be taught. If they are open to learning, then take them on because they can turn into a valuable part of your team.

Agents are sales people. In the early 2000s, everybody was making a ton of money in real estate. People who wanted the same things you want—more time, more money, more freedom, more security— thought real estate was for them. However, if you don't like sales, then real estate isn't a sweet spot for you because whether you're an investor, agent or broker, you must do something with sales. In real estate, about 10% of the agents are grabbing 90% of all the sales. The other 10% of the agents, you can see at the movie theater on a Tuesday at 1:30 p.m. because they are not selling any real estate. It's not that they are bad; it's just that the business doesn't suit them.

Terence

I have been a licensed Realtor since 1997, and I have worked in numerous brokerages. I have been in boutique offices as well as a large 100-agent office, I have had my own mid-sized RE/MAX office, and I have worked with hundreds of agents on transactions over the years.

What I have learned from all of this is that agents are people. They have strengths and weaknesses. They don't have all the answers; they are not all-powerful and all-knowing; they are human. Unfortunately, because of the nature of the real estate business, they are probably a little more human than most. There are high-achieving motivated agents, but the industry as a whole does draw a lot of people who want "flexibility," which is another way of saying they want to work 12 hours a week and get paid full time for doing it.

In my peak years working as a traditional agent, I often worked 50 to 60 hours a week and was usually lucky to grab lunch at a drive-thru. On many days, there was just no time to eat. It was a busy real estate market, and I didn't want any business to slip through my fingers.

I finally did get a little burned out, so I decided to open my own brokerage, hoping that I could leverage other agents' time and spend more of my time with my three young children. I grew to just over 20 agents at the peak of the market in 2006.

Did my plan work? Were there lots of anxious, motivated agents running around busily working 50 to 60 hours a week as I had done? Sadly, there were not. Instead, on many days I would look around the office and wonder how my secretary and I were the only ones in the office on a Wednesday at 11 a.m. Were they all out working hard and showing property or taking new listings? Again, sadly, they were not. Out of the 20 agents, there were three or four motivated, efficient and successful agents who handled 70% to 80% of the transaction volume for the office. The rest had "flexible" schedules and did three to four properties a year if they were lucky. That volume of business does not give you enough experience to know the market or understand the lending process, or the expertise to effectively negotiate a sale.

So was I just terrible at recruiting agents and got the bottom of the barrel? Nope. This is the norm in every real estate office in America, and probably, the world. According to the National Association of Realtors, there are just over two million licensed real estate agents in the US, and as I write this, there were just over five million sales of new and existing homes, meaning that the average licensed Realtor handles fewer than five transaction sides or sales per year.

Most of our colleagues handle 20 to 30 sales a year, and one friend will do over 200 sales this year with the help of two other licensed buyers' agents and several assistants, so how is this possible? A lot of people who hold licenses aren't working in the business. But there are also tens of thousands of Realtors who despite having so much flexibility, somehow manage to bump into four transactions per year. Do they treasure those four properties so much that they do an exceptional job with marketing and make themselves available at all times to get these houses sold? Of course not. You will be lucky to get a return call from these guys within a week.

Why are we telling you this? Because before you find your ideal agent, you need to know that these tens, maybe hundreds of thousands of unqualified agents are out there. Avoid them at all costs. You will meet these agents, and they will seem very nice, and you will think, well, our kids go to school together, or we share a love of golf, and it will seem natural to hire them to sell your next project. Or maybe it's your brother-in-law, or brother, or best friend. But if they are not full-time, dedicated to making their living through selling real estate, and have at least a few years' experience with, and passionate about learning everything they can about the business, do not hire them! Again, do not hire them!

Choose the Right Balance

You need to find a full-time professional who has worked with contractors, understands what you do, and knows the market. It's great to have a valid second opinion when it comes to doing improvements or marketing or pricing the home. If you have a great contractor and a great agent, now you have a valid second and third opinion. The more, the better.

So if you pick the ideal, most qualified, and successful agent in your market, is it going to be easy to sell your properties? Will you just get to sit back and wait for the checks to roll in? Maybe, but not likely. You don't want to pick the busiest Realtor in your town. He or she has staff and is dealing with volume, so even if you give them eight to 10 listings per year, they are not set up to give individualized attention. You might not fit into their box or be what their three transaction coordinators are used to dealing with. And you will rarely get your superstar Realtor on the phone.

Because they are going for volume, they are also typically looking to price homes below the market average, so their listings sell more quickly. One of our friends who is a very successful Realtor spends every Monday making price-reduction calls to his sellers. If you are trying to sell 200 homes a year, every price reduction of $5,000 to $10,000 is going to help you avoid expired listings or long marketing times, but is it the best solution for those sellers? Possibly for the ones who overpriced the houses from the beginning, but for you, the investor, shaving your prices by an extra $5,000 to $10,000 or more per house can cost you half your potential income.

We have talked about balancing on the razor's edge when it comes to finding your contractor, and the same holds true with finding your perfect Realtor. You want the successful Realtor who has tons of market knowledge but isn't so busy that he can't take your call or has such a large team that she always pawns you off to an inexperienced underling.

If you did what you were supposed to do in the earlier chapters, by now you have met or even taken five to 10 Realtors to lunch or coffee, so hopefully you have gotten to know a few of them. As you prepare your first house for the market, it's time to start asking Realtors pointed questions. How many homes do they sell each year on average? What have they found to be the most successful techniques to market these homes? Do they have a website? Do they do open houses? Do they advertise? Do they use a professional photographer or drone photography for homes with acreage? Are they available to handle offers on the weekends? Try to figure out how they get along with other agents.

Ask for Referrals

Referrals are a great way to find great agents or inexperienced agents you can train, whether those referrals come from another investor who does a lot of properties or from an escrow, title, or mortgage person. It is crucial because you don't know if the agent you are meeting with is doing three to four contracts a year, 10 contracts a year, or 100 contracts a year. You really should ask your escrow officers what they think of the agents before you hire them; they usually know their dark side if they have one.

Jerry

Different real estate chains post the awards and production levels of their agents, which can give you an idea of who is doing what. What I would do with Terence was call and say, for example, "Terence, I'm looking for some investment properties in Park City. Can you find me a viable agent?" Then he could check who was selling a lot of properties. Other agents can do this as well. At least it lets you know that you are dealing with someone who has handled some transactions.

If you call any real estate office in America, there is a high probability of getting an agent handling "floor duty," which means they get all the incoming calls for a certain shift. While experienced agents can take the floor, more often than not, especially in larger chain offices, you are getting newer agents who are trying to grow their business. You don't want to be part of their learning curve!

Terence has found quality agents for dozens of people in about 20 different states for single-family, multi-family, and commercial properties. In fact, a good friend who got into investing through us got connected with an experienced Realtor in Los Angeles via Terence. He was able to buy investment property a few years ago, did extremely well with it, and went on to buy another investment property in Chicago that also worked out very well.

Now he's using some of that equity to renovate a home in California with more to come in the next few months—all from a 20-minute conversation about his needs and goals and some research into which Realtors would be the best counterparts for what he was trying to do. This is a great resource we offer. It costs you nothing, so visit our website www.flippingmainstreet.com and take advantage of this great service today if you need a jumpstart in your market.

Be Realistic

Now let's talk about your expectations to make sure you know what you are hiring the Realtor to do—and to make sure you know what you are supposed to be doing to make this process work well for everyone.

If the comps show that your home is worth $225,000, yet you "really need to sell it for $250,000," you can't expect that your Realtor is going to drop everything to start marketing this house or that he or she has a magic sales plan to get this house in escrow in 15 days. Your house is going to sit for three to four weeks, and your agent will try to please you by starting out hopeful before gradually sharing feedback and eventually telling you the truth that your house needs to be priced at $225,000 to $229,000 to get any showing activity or offers. You will either get mad at the agent and feel like he or she is not doing their job or grudgingly reduce the price, probably only to $239,900. Then you start the process over, so in another three to four weeks, you will either fire your agent when they "haven't done their job," or you will reduce to $229,900 and get that $225,000 offer.

Because your property has now been on the market for eight weeks, agents might also stop showing it or think there is something wrong, so you might be reducing to $219,000 at the 12-week mark and taking $215,000 with a closing cost credit and hating your agent or telling them they need to cut their commission to make the offer work.

Now they have wasted 12 extra weeks with you, had six to 12 awkward phone conversations, and lost half of their commission, and they have another unhappy client out there telling the community what a terrible job they did. Do you think they are going to want to list your next project? Or better yet, do you think they will bring you that smoking hot deal that the agent in the next cubicle is listing next week? Never.

Remember, if you buy your homes right, you can sell your homes right. And if you can sell your homes right, you will sell more homes, and your agent or agents will love you. Then if they hear about a great opportunity, you are going to be the first to hear about it.

Agents can only sell homes at market value, or on a good day, for maybe 2% or 3% over current market value, so don't have ridiculous expectations. If they prepare a solid CMA (Comparative Market Analysis) that shows that your price is $225,000, and your gut is telling you that this is your price too, then don't be ridiculous and price it $30,000 higher just because you would like to make that extra money. If you don't have the right experienced agent, they might undershoot the market, but typically they are going to be pretty close.

Complete the Project First

Once your property looks great, the utilities are on, and the staging is complete, then and only then can you invite the agent and his or her photographer out to the house. Think back to what we talked about in the last chapter and remember not to get anxious. Don't let the agent come out until the house is ready to sell. If they give you advice on what upgrades to make or give you feedback on the project along the way, that's great, but don't let them rush you at the end because they are anxious for a listing. Make sure that you do your blue tape, your finishes and cleaning, and great staging, and that the yard is polished, and every scrap of construction debris is offsite before you have them come out to list the property.

Agents are all about momentum, so if you have them come out with their photographer and the pictures look awful with waist-high weeds, unfinished fencing, and missing fixtures, the odds of getting the photographer back a second time are nil. Agents don't like to pay for anything, so they don't want to pay another $75 when they have already paid once. Do your job so they can do theirs.

Also, agents are not immune to emotion. Most of the houses they list have a few stains on the carpet, a litter box in the laundry room, and a few fogged windows or dirty dishes in the sink, so if they walk into your latest project, and it is *perfect,* they are going to be excited. Then when you tell them you would be thrilled to get the $225,000, they might be so fired up that they list it at $235,000, get their whole office out for the weekly office caravan, and sell it for the $235,000 in a week. This will happen when you buy your houses right and do your job.

Your Job and Your Agent's Job

So what if your contractor has done a great job of polishing up everything, but you left the 30-year-old air conditioner on the roof and didn't get a pest inspection, and now you are three weeks into escrow, and the buyers' agent asks for a new HVAC system at $7,500 and $6,000 worth of dry rot and termite spraying under the house? Is this your agent's fault? Have they somehow not done their job, or should they be able to expertly negotiate you out of this $13,500 mess? Should the two agents give up their commissions to make the offer work? Are these buyers being unreasonable?

Know what your job is and what the agent's job is. The agent's job is to sell the house, but they can't sell something that can't be financed or wasn't ready to sell in the first place. Now the buyers are worried about the other problems you might have covered up, so even if you agree to fix these things, it might be too late. You have broken the buyers' trust, so they cancel anyway. Now you are back on the market. The house is a little stigmatized since it fell out of escrow, and instead of selling for that awesome $235,000, you are back to selling for $219,000 12 weeks from now.

The listing appointment with the Realtor is the time to set some expectations. If you have used this Realtor twenty times, you will probably have your system down, but if it's a new agent to you, make sure you put your expectations in writing in the listing agreement before you and he or she sign it.

Terence

Though most listing agreements don't put the agents' responsibilities in writing, we highly recommend that you require them to do so. The basic boilerplate of the listing agreement tells you that they are going to be "diligent" but beyond that, it typically only states that they are going to install a sign and lockbox and put the property on the MLS.

The following should be in your listing contract before you sign:

The agent will:

- Create glossy fliers
- Install a flier box and keep it stocked at least every three days
- Host a broker's open house
- Have at least two open houses per month until the property sells

The listing will be on:

- Their website
- Zillow
- Trulia
- Realtor.com
- Craigslist with high-res photographs and a virtual tour
- PayShow if it is available in their area
- Facebook
- Instagram

When your pen is poised two inches above that listing agreement, most agents will agree to almost anything to get the listing signed.

Your best move is not to push for expensive and typically ineffective advertising in newspapers or magazines. If you do have PayShow in your market, both you and your agent should contribute fees toward the service. In the interest of full disclosure, PayShow is a new service we have developed to help agents, buyers, and sellers get more out of the real estate experience. You can check it out at www.payshow.com.

Other than that, grass-root methods are more effective. It doesn't cost agents a lot to print or stock fliers, get good photographs, host open houses, or periodically check to make sure your listings are showing up on the top sites. Nevertheless, these are the activities that ensure that any active buyers and agents in the market know about your property.

If you don't have a photographer using a drone in your market, we highly recommend buying one yourself. For properties on large lots, they create a fantastic presentation. The drone can also be walked through the house without its rotors for an amazing first-person virtual home tour. When you have this kind of presentation uploaded to Zillow, your agent's website, and the MLS, it creates instant credibility for your home and makes even an entry-level house feel high end. If you operate the drone yourself, this is going to cost you next to nothing and is going to be a great aid to your Realtor and to getting your house sold.

Also, contribute toward the costs and efforts of the broker's open house and any other open houses. Make sure the house is clean and ready for open houses, put out bottled water or snacks and drinks for the broker's open house and maybe even a few Starbucks cards to encourage as many agents as possible to walk through. Agents need to be inspired; they won't leave the office to advance their careers or build their market knowledge, but they will leave the office for a $5 Starbucks card, and in the process, they will realize they might actually have a buyer for your home.

Prepare your agent in advance to bring all the appropriate disclosures with them to the listing appointment and ideally meet at the house. If you complete these disclosures together at the house, you can make sure that the details are accurate. If you are working on multiple projects, it's very easy to forget whether a house has an electric or gas-fired stove or furnace or water heater, which rooms have exhaust fans, or if there is 220 wiring in the garage, kitchen, or laundry room. With the agent and all the disclosures in hand, you should be able to complete this appointment in less than 30 minutes. Then you will be completely done with this property. With a clear pest report, well inspection, septic inspection, and all the disclosures uploaded in the MLS with your listing, there is nothing left for your agent to do but market the house and get it sold for top dollar. This makes their job so easy that they may even offer a better discount on the next one.

You must manage the agent, since in most cases their broker certainly isn't managing them. If they have to scramble around at the last minute to get disclosures together, it makes it stressful for everyone. If you don't have to be involved in anything other than contract negotiations, you will have that much more time to find the next project or the next lender to expand your business.

In a perfect world, you will find that motivated, sincere and experienced agent who is happy to help with a little light staging and will hold 10 open houses and advertise the house on every page of the local real estate magazine. But more than likely, you are going to find a good agent, who is human, whose real job is to put the home effectively on the local Multiple Listing Service; be available for calls; help you price the home correctly; handle contracts, disclosures, and inspections; and ideally give you a modest discount for what they hope will be a volume relationship. If you do your job, you will allow them to do theirs, and you will become their favorite client. They will become involved in your success, they will find you opportunities, and everyone will make money and have a good time doing it.

A note on for sale by owners or licensed flippers: If you market your homes, or your agent is a family member or a part of your team, everything we just talked about still applies, but even more so. Sometimes agents will do more work for a new client or stranger than they will do for their family or friends. They think they can get away with more if it's family because they know they won't be fired. It's easy to be your own worst boss or your spouse's worst boss. It can make for a very awkward date night if you have just lectured your husband about not getting the house on the MLS or getting the sign up.

Make sure you treat yourself like a client; be a good boss, even to yourself. If you have a license but don't handle any sales or know the contracts or pricing, you will be very well served by paying an agent who does know about these things.

> ## Terence
> I have a good friend who has been a licensed broker for 20 years but does mostly hard money lending. For the last eight years, I have listed all his properties for him. I know he doesn't like paying for it, but he knows that he doesn't know the market or the business like I do. If you're not the professional, make sure you find one.

If you need help finding an agent, visit www.flippingmainstreet.com and we will get to work finding you the perfect agent in your market.

If you think your agent is going to wave a magic wand and sell your house for you, then you are going to have many harsh lessons. When you do your job on the front end, it makes your agent's job super easy.

When you start to do deals with agents, and they see that you are serious, then the agents in the middle range, not those who do 200 or 50 contracts a year, but pros who do 20 to 30 properties a year and understand your market will seek you out, bring you opportunities, and go the extra mile for you because you go the extra mile for them.

If you decide not to use an agent and decide to be a For Sale by Owner instead, you are going down a road that will eventually bring you less money and less time. You will be dealing more in a wholesale market rather than a retail market, so you will have to do more volume to make the same amount of money. Our goal for you is that you make more money using less of your time. The way to do that is to buy—not sell—in the wholesale market, and sell—not buy—in the retail market.

CHAPTER 11

THE ESCROW PART II

It seems like this next step in the process should be easy, but without planning it can be the most stressful, most demoralizing, and most expensive part of the entire process, so let's get it right the first time.

People assume it should be easy because they think "I already did all the paperwork when I bought the house, so I should have everything" or "I'll just let the agent figure everything out; after all, that's what I'm paying him for." Didn't you read the last few chapters? We want everyone doing the functions at which they excel, and for most agents, that isn't paperwork, follow-through, or even marketing. Now you might be confused, but remember that agents are just functionaries to give you some second opinions, get your homes on the MLS, and provide a very useful buffer between you and the buyers and the buyers' agent. You can help your agent and yourself through this resale escrow process by doing a few key things.

Get the House Perfect and Keep It That Way

Let's start with the house. This is the part where you make sure not to get overanxious and let the agent list the house before the contractor is finished. Many agents will push for this, or they will tell you, "It looks amazing. Let's get it on for the weekend and not miss out on all those buyers and the good weather." But as we talked about earlier, if it's still missing mirrors and has dirty screens, has a pile of dead brush and old deck boards in the side yard, you are going to miss the good buyers anyway. Or if you get the good buyers, they're definitely not going to give you the price you want. Spend that extra time and burn through your roll of blue tape to make sure the house is perfect before allowing the agent through the front door. In some cases, we might even caution you not to let the agent see the house while it's under renovation as this might dampen their enthusiasm. You want the magic of your renovation to affect even your listing agent, but if they see the stained carpets and gross cabinets on the front end, the memory of those things might lessen their enthusiasm when they see it finished.

An easy way to prepare for your resale escrow is to pretend that you are the buyers or the buyers' agent. Go through our Resale Escrow Checklist at the end of this chapter, and walk in the buyers' or buyers' agent's footsteps for a while. Start by simply walking through your newly finished project and try to turn on the air-conditioning, turn on the stove, and turn on all the lights to see how many bulbs are either missing or burned out. Light bulbs, blue tape, 9-volt batteries, caulking, a flashlight, a screwdriver, Windex, paper towels, toilet paper, and a few carbon monoxide and smoke detectors are always good to have on hand. Keep going through the house, run every faucet and the garbage disposal, and open and close cupboards and doors to see what latches and what doesn't. Sit on the toilets and make sure they don't wobble or rock. Loose toilets are common, and you don't want the first time the new owners sit on the toilet in their new home to be a bad experience.

Terence

Walk on the carpet in your socks. I had renovated a house that was very high-end for me, on acreage in a great school district, and it even came with a guesthouse. I walked the house with my contractor in my socks, and something poked my foot. It turned out to be a ring full of keys, right under the carpet and pad in the middle of the living room floor! Don't ask me how the carpet installer got home that day, but obviously, he had to make an emergency trip back to my project to lift the carpet, remove the foreign object, and re-stretch the carpet. Imagine if prospective buyers had stepped on that or found that after the close of escrow. Would they feel like they were buying a quality home or that a reputable contractor had done the work? Mistakes certainly happen, but your job is finding them before prospective buyers or their agents do.

Agents love to find flaws and point out poor workmanship. They are torn between justifying their existence and talking their clients out of a sale, but ego always prevails, so they start badmouthing the property just to show off their knowledge. Don't give them a chance. If you win the agents over, and it looks like an easy escrow for them, they will start singing your home's praises! Remember, they don't want to open an escrow that is going to cancel when the buyers find a bunch of problems, so if they start seeing red flags, they are going to cart those buyers away to the next property.

Make it easy for them. Walk in your socks. Use the garage door opener and make sure it works and doesn't sound like a thousand squeaky hinges. Maybe add WD-40 to your bag of tricks. Every husband in America is going to hit that button and open that garage door while his wife and the agent are looking at the rest of the home. They just can't resist. So if it's not connected, jams halfway, or squeals like a piggy, your chances of a sale just got cut in half. Your chances of a full price offer went to nil.

Jerry

If you have a lot of tech with buttons in the house, make sure it works because men like to push those buttons as well. I had a home in Park City where the vent for the stove came up from the counter by the push of a button—a terrible invention all around. When I pushed the button, it came up and spewed grease and dirt all over the stove. Great, I thought, I get to lower my asking price. The next thing is jetted bathtubs. *Do not put them in!* They break easily and rarely work. Simple, clean and new often outshines high-tech, complicated and problematic.

Make sure there aren't a hundred pieces of painter's tape, rusty screws, and paint chips from when the painter power washed the house lying all over the yard. Also, make sure someone is doing weekly yard maintenance for the duration of your escrow. Countless times, we have seen both investors and regular sellers get their properties in escrow and promptly stop taking care of the yards. It makes for very bad feelings when the buyers show up for inspections, or with their moving trucks, and the yards are either overgrown or dead.

The same goes for cleaning. If the house has been on the market for a few months and you take a 60-day escrow, get a cleaner to go back through. It's disappointing for buyers when they do their final walk through, and there are cobwebs, dead bugs, and dust all over their future home. I just sent my awesome cleaner back through a house prior to the closing. Her bill was $37.50—so well worth it to have the buyers move in and feel like they're moving in to a new home. Don't be stingy.

Make sure the trash cans are emptied. The contractors have probably hauled away all the demo trash, but now their cleaners and yard guys have thrown fast food wrappers and half-empty Red Bull cans in the trash can for six weeks without taking the can to the curb. It's 100 degrees, and now the whole side yard smells like a landfill.

If it's an REO and the trash cans had trash in them for a year, call the city or trash company and get them to swap out the cans. You don't want the new buyers to move in and be completely revolted on their first time taking out the trash. It's all psychology. They see that filthy interior of the trash can, and for the first time, they forget about all your beautiful finishes and start worrying about what slobs were living in the house they thought was their dream home. Don't ruin the experience for them.

Put yourself in the buyers' shoes and examine everything with a critical eye. Imagine that you are paying your full sales price. Would it be worth it to you?

Stay on Top of the Utilities

This may sound simple, and we have talked about it before, but please make sure that the home has all the utilities on and that all appliances are up and running. This includes having the pilot light lit in the furnace and water heater and making sure that the new stove is attached to the gas line. For country properties, if you have a propane tank, make sure it has been filled and isn't locked off or missing a connector. You would be surprised how often you can work on a late spring or summer rehab, and since no one has thought about heat or turning on the stove during the remodel, you suddenly get to inspections and find out that the propane company isn't servicing your part of the county for two weeks. Or it's the middle of winter, and they finally got around to removing the tank on the REO property you bought because no one paid the bill that has been outstanding for two years. Now it's near freezing, and you have no heat source and $4,000 in new plumbing to worry about. These are the easy little things that become big issues and sleepless nights if not addressed or planned for ahead of time.

Utilities can be confusing. You might have one utility company for electric and one for gas, a waste management company for trash collection, and a local water district for water. That adds up to four different monthly bills just for utilities on one house, which is why you need to stay on top of the little things.

Please visit our website www.flippingmainstreet.com for a printable Monthly Bill Checklist that we use to keep up on all the important bills and inspections during our remodels. Print it out and put it in your construction and accounting folders in your remodel binder, and use it for each of your projects. This will also help you to notice any discrepancies that could be costing you extra money.

> ## Terence
>
> I recently had a house where the landscaper cranked the sprinklers up for the new sod. No one ever turned them back down, and what should have been a $40 water bill was $280 the next month. At least I caught it the first month instead of three months later.

Also, if home inspectors show up to inspect the house, and there is no gas or water, they are going to leave, someone is going to have to pay a re-inspection fee, and you will probably have to wait a week to get them back out.

The same thing just happened to a contractor/investor friend of ours. He was selling one of his flip properties and claimed that the well had been working fine, but on the day that both the well and septic inspector showed up, the well wouldn't work. A week later, he still hadn't even gotten the estimate back from the well company on what it was going to take to fix the well, let alone get those two inspections rescheduled.

The well probably hadn't been working for months, and if he had been checking the property thoroughly, he could have had it fixed and ready to go. Instead he is paying 12% on an $118,000 loan and other costs that look like this:

Interest: $40 per day

+ Property tax: $3 per day

+ Utility costs: $7 per day
+ Insurance costs: $7 per day
+ Maintenance costs: $3 per day
= $60 per day!

If it takes two weeks to get those inspectors back, he has just lost another $840!

$60 per day x 14 days = $840

All this because he didn't go by the house, which is less than four miles from his home. This is the easy $1,000 per hour money. Five to six extra visits of five minutes each to save $840—it's a no-brainer.

The lender he uses, like most private lenders, allows him to borrow about $250,000 at a time. Most of the opportunities he has been looking for will take close to $200,000 to acquire and rehab, so until he gets this one off the books, he is stalled from doing any more projects with that lender. When you take into account the opportunity cost as well, it really starts to hurt.

You may think that when you do a lot of properties, you are bound to run into a few problems or have a little waste. Or you may think that you don't want to focus on the small picture because you are a big-picture person. We are big picture people too, but if you don't manage your small picture, it will become big picture in a hurry. When you get to doing 20 or more properties a year and realize that by making a lot of little mistakes you are losing $5,000 to $8,000 per house, that is a six-figure mistake, and it was all avoidable with the right oversight and systems in place. It's all in the preparation and planning. Use the Monthly Bill Checklist that you can find on our website.

Jerry

Low-hanging fruit tastes just as good as the ones at the top of the tree.

Know the Requirements

This is also where you must consult with your agent and make sure you know about any requirements for FHA, VA, USDA, or other government-sponsored loan programs or area requirements that might exist in your market.

A Crash Course on Government-Insured Loans

VA stands for Veterans Administration, which insures VA loans for veterans. These loans offer very favorable terms. It's one of the only loans where the buyer can put no money down, with typically no mortgage insurance, which is a huge benefit. The loan includes other provisions that disallow the buyer from paying for certain fees associated with the escrow, including the pest inspection and some escrow costs, so pay attention to these requirements when making counter offers for VA buyers.

FHA stands for Federal Housing Administration, which are government insured loans most often used by first-time buyers. These loans can be used for any buyers who are buying a home they intend to live in if they meet a few other minimal requirements. Typically, FHA makes it easier for low-income buyers or buyers with mediocre credit. They will also finance buyers only two years out of bankruptcy and three years out of a foreclosure or short sale. These are typically 3.5% down loans, but despite the fact that they have low down payments and easier qualification requirements, they are not great loans because they do have very expensive mortgage insurance premiums. Then again, if you have had a bankruptcy and you want to buy a house again, this may be your only option.

VA and FHA appraisers are a little more stringent than conventional appraisers. If they notice peeling paint or dry rot, they are obligated to note that in their appraisal. The property must have a working stove and floor coverings, and there must be an operable heat source.

If you have done a top-notch renovation, you should have no problem working with VA and FHA buyers. They will sometimes pay a premium because some sellers do not like working with these loans because they take longer to close. Also, because some of these buyers have marginal income, employment history, and credit history, these transactions have a higher rate of failure. You are also dealing with clients who have no money or very limited funds to use for the purchase, so if a major issue is found and needs to be negotiated, they have nothing to contribute. Plan accordingly, but keep in mind that nearly half of our sales are made with FHA, VA, and USDA buyers, which are all government-insured loans. Welcome to America.

Terence

In my market, we are required to have smoke detectors, carbon monoxide detectors, and water heater strapping in place before any sale. While cash buyers can ignore these items, if I sell to financed buyers and those items are not in place when the appraiser comes through, it costs an extra $75 to $100 for a re-inspection. And it typically delays the sale up to a week while we wait for the appraiser to come back through. I learned long ago to make sure the contractor had all these items completed in advance.

If you keep the existing smoke detectors, please make sure to put new batteries in them. Who knows how many millions of dollars have been lost because of a smoke detector chirping a low battery warning during a home showing. It's impossible to get comfortable in a house with something ringing in your ear every 30 seconds.

During your renovation, or ideally before buying the home, you should have had your own home inspector and pest inspector go through the home. As we said in earlier chapters, we recommend clearing the termite or pest work before going back on the market.

> ## Terence
> In my market, nearly half of the buyers are VA or FHA buyers and must have a clear pest inspection for their financing, so if I can market up front that the house already has a clear pest report, it makes it that much easier for their agent.

Get the Reports Up Front

One of the hardest issues to handle in any escrow is negotiating pest work that was unknown at the time of the original offer negotiation. Agents know this, and most dread dealing with this since it typically leaves everyone feeling put out, so if they know they won't have to deal with that issue, your house has just become much more attractive.

This is also a time issue. We discussed earlier that it could take one to two weeks to get a pest inspector out to the property, a few days to get a complicated report back, a few days to wait for the buyers' agent to put their request for repairs together, and another one to three weeks to schedule and complete the work. In a worst-case scenario, if the agent waited two weeks even to call the pest company, just this part of the escrow could be six to seven weeks from start to finish. At 12% interest, vacant property insurance rates, taxes, and maintenance, you have just cost yourself thousands of dollars for nothing. Why not clear the report on the front end? You know that 80% of the time, you must do this work anyway.

Also, if you have never had anyone go under your 1950s "charming bungalow" and have no idea of what is under there, it is going to be extremely nerve-wracking when the buyers' pest inspector suits up to crawl it. You won't know if it's dry as a bone with no damage or a $20,000 nightmare. That is not a fun way to do business, so make sure to do your homework early.

The same applies if the property is out in the country and has a well and septic. Get these reports up front. In most cases, your agent can upload these reports right into their MLS listing. Some investors are afraid it will scare away buyers, and that can happen, but only if you didn't do the work like you were supposed to. In that case, it is better to scare them away early than have them tie up the property for three to four weeks and then cancel.

Be on Time

Investors love to complain about contractors who don't finish their work, but investors are even worse about leaving things undone and racing off to find the next project. So set a good example for your contractors and agents by getting all of your work done on the front end. Make sure the professionals in your market talk about you as someone who values their time and almost always has everything buttoned up for every escrow you do with them. Don't make yourself known as a buffoon who is never ready. It makes the buyers and the buyers' agent more comfortable if they feel like they are receiving everything in a timely manner. Please visit our website www.flippingmainstreet.com for ways to help with overload and to make sure you can manage what is on your plate so you can be that investor who everyone says is on time and prepared.

Terence

Before I had my systems in place, I would procrastinate on my disclosures or inspections, and yes, I confess again that I put houses on the market that weren't ready for prime time. It seemed ridiculous to me at the time, but I lost a few escrows because I didn't get the disclosures to the buyers in a timely fashion. I thought, the house is perfect, and there is nothing to disclose, so what does it matter? But the buyers and their inexperienced agent probably thought I was disorganized or had something I was trying to hide from them.

First-time buyers think everyone—their lender, the inspectors and contractors, their agent, the listing agent, and especially the seller—is out to get them. If you give them any chance to bolt, they are going to take it. Treat them like skittish little animals. Gently lure them in with something shiny, don't make any sudden or surprising movements, and eventually soothe them into such a state of calm that the escrow closes without them ever having to feel nervous or uncertain.

Minimize Delays

After making sure that you are doing everything on time, your final and maybe most important task during this escrow period is to follow up with everyone else involved in the transaction to ensure that they are doing everything right and on time. We saw earlier how eight different subcontractors could add a month to a project by each one just getting a couple of days behind, and the same is true with the vendors involved with your escrow. We have eliminated half of the major delays by providing inspections and clearances up front, which is huge. But if there is a loan involved, which there will be most of the time, there are still lots of opportunities for delays. So here is how to stop or at least minimize them.

When you receive the initial offer, make sure there is a pre-qualification or preapproval letter included. Have your agent get straightforward answers from the lender on whether they have pulled the buyers' credit, verified employment, and provided the buyers with a good faith estimate that shows what they will need for a down payment and what their future payment will be. It is best to say no to somebody who is putting no money down, delivers newspapers for a living, and has a credit score of 450 because the house is most likely going to fall out of escrow, and you will waste the time of everyone involved.

The lending industry is still completely unregulated, despite what anyone says, and it is shocking how often lenders will "prequalify" buyers based on a 90-second phone conversation. We have seen buyers get six weeks into escrows in which both they and the sellers have spent hundreds of dollars on inspections, appraisals, and repairs only to find that the lenders missed the little detail that the buyers' bankruptcy or previous foreclosure was still too recent, or that they had unpaid child support liens, bad credit, or were still on a home or car loan with their previous spouse. It happens all the time; so the more you can push or have your agent push on the buyers' lender the better. The lender is the biggest piece of this puzzle, so make sure everyone is making the lender's life miserable until he gets the loan funded.

You should also push for the appraisal to be ordered as quickly as possible and should even stipulate this in the contract, like "buyer to pay for and order appraisal within three days of acceptance." This can't be done if the buyers haven't done inspections or don't have disclosures or reports on the house, but if you have done your upfront work, the buyers should have had all these materials before they even wrote an offer, so now they should feel comfortable paying for the appraisal. This will also push their lender to do their upfront homework to make sure that the buyers are worthy borrowers.

If the buyers ask for a laundry list of repairs or credits after your perfect renovation (How dare they!), what do you do? First, what is the market cycle? Is it a buyer's or a seller's market? How long did it take to get the house under contract? Were there multiple offers? Did you already reduce far below asking price or give large buyer closing cost credit? Remember that there is always a cost and a stigma to going back on the market. So if it's going to cost you $5,000 or $8,000 to go back on the market, and the buyers are asking for $3,000 worth of repairs and they are ready to close in two weeks, a child could figure out the answer. Keep your emotions out of it, do the work, and close the escrow. Remember basic math. Conversely, if there was a lot of interest and multiple offers, you went under contract quickly, and the buyers are demanding, get rid of them quickly and move on. If you do agree to make repairs, get the written list to your contractor immediately and just like at the beginning of your rehab, walk the project with him so you are on the same page. Bring your blue tape to make sure he doesn't replace the wrong fogged window.

> ## Jerry
> Terence has been the buffer for me on so many rants while in es-
> crow that I have stopped counting—rants that, if I had been han-
> dling dealing with a buyer or seller directly, I could have harmed
> the outcome. That is why I like to have an agent between myself
> and the offer. The agent isn't as emotionally attached to the project
> as you and usually gives the much-needed beat before contacting
> the other side in an open escrow. If you do choose to do your own
> selling, make sure you have a sounding board when things get frus-
> trating, and give yourself time before responding to things that put
> you in reaction.

Make sure your agent has received the receipt for the buyers' earnest
money deposit and that the escrow has been opened. Ask your agent
for the escrow number, so you know it has been done. Then push to
make sure they are getting the preliminary title report.

Keep the buyers' agent to tight timeframes. Remember this is costing you money every day, so one extra week in escrow could be $300
to $600, plus the possibility of not having your money reloaded for the
next good opportunity.

Another way to keep the pressure on is to enforce a penalty if the
escrow closes after a specified date. If everyone but the lender has
done their work, and the lender is dropping the ball, it will typically
be the lender paying this penalty. Also, with this penalty hanging over
their heads, that first-time buyer couple will be sure to get their lender
whatever documentation he asks for in a hurry. Lenders typically ask
for extra items or items for clarification four to five times during an
escrow, so if the buyers take two to three days each time to get their
paperwork in, this can add up to a lot of wasted time. At a daily penalty
of $50 to $100, this will keep the buyers on a tighter leash.

Title and escrow people must be pushed as well. Always tell them
that you want a "rush." Otherwise, they can get complacent, and they
usually have a stack of 20 files in front of them. Keep yours at the top

of the heap by being or making your agent the squeaky wheel. This doesn't mean pester them, waste their time, or ever speak rudely to them, but touch base regularly via email to ensure that there is steady movement.

Terence

I love my title and escrow people and think they are the hardest working people in real estate. At the same time, I have been baffled hundreds of times in my career when escrow officers ask me, "When are we trying to close?" Huh? The first page of the contract says in clear writing February 21, and they are asking me 40 days into escrow on February 19 when we want to close. It's weird but true. You have to monitor and encourage them like everyone else.

If you are taking any long vacations or going out of town, make sure the escrow officers know so they can get you in to sign before you leave. The last thing you want is to be the one who holds up your own escrow and paycheck.

Without supervision, an escrow can easily drag out to 60 or 75 days, and at the daily rate we saw earlier, you can see how a lack of structure and planning can cost $100,000 per year. And if you run your escrows wrong, you will be doing two to three escrows on the same house, which becomes exhausting and expensive. But if you stay on top of everyone, there is no reason you can't close escrow within 30 days, provided the lender has done his homework on the buyers before they started shopping. Do it right, do it once, and as Terence's dad always says, "The only good escrow is a closed escrow."

RESALE ESCROW CHECKLIST

1.   Make sure escrow is opened:

    a. You have received the buyers' deposit check.

    b. You have provided the escrow officer with a complete contract with any and all addenda and counteroffers.

    c. You have provided the escrow officer with your current lender's name and contact information.

    d. You have contacted your private lender and let them know the property is in escrow and the projected close of escrow date.

2. Make sure the buyers' lender has the completed purchase agreement and all pertinent addenda or counteroffers. (Yes, this is the buyers' agent's job, but it's your time that is going to be wasted if they take three days plus a long weekend to send the contract over.)

    Ask them very directly when the appraisal will be ordered, and schedule another call for that date to make sure that it has been ordered. The lender will tell you that they don't want to risk the buyers' $450 until they get their file in order, so make sure they know that it costs you $60 per day in interest, utilities, taxes, and insurance while the property is in escrow. Lenders and buyers often forget that escrows cost sellers money as well.

3. If you have inspection reports and clearances from your acquisition file:

    a. Immediately provide these to the buyers' agent.

    b. Immediately provide completed disclosures.

Ideally, these documents will be provided to prospective buyers prior to accepting their contract or even prior to them writing an offer if uploaded to the MLS listing. If a buyer has an issue with something in the disclosures or reports, better they never even waste your time than tie the property up for three weeks and then cancel based on the disclosures or inspections.

4. Prepare for the buyers' inspections and appraisal:

    a. Revisit your property with fresh eyes and go through your pre-sale process all over again.

        1. All utilities are on.
        2. All appliances turn on and work.
        3. All light fixtures have bulbs.
        4. All faucets run with hot and cold water.
        5. All toilets flush.
        6. The garage door opens.
        7. Smoke detectors and CO detectors are installed and working.
        8. If the home has been sitting vacant, send the cleaner back through to re-vacuum, dust, wipe down surfaces, and remove any trash or leftover construction debris.

    b. Make sure that your property receives regular attention and that everything looks in peak condition.

        1. Maintain the yard.
        2. Blow away leaves.
        3. If there is a pool, regularly maintain the pool.
        4. Make sure the thermostat is maintained at a comfortable level.

5.   Stay in regular contact with all parties:

   a. Your escrow officer

      1. Make weekly progress monitoring calls.
      2. Make sure that they have ordered a loan payoff from your current lender and that your lender is available to sign. You don't want to get close to the end of your escrow and find out that your private lender is on a three-week African safari.

   b. Your agent

      1. Make sure the disclosures have been reviewed by the buyers and the buyers' agent and returned with signatures.
      2. If the buyers are having inspections, make sure that they have been ordered and that there is easy access with a lockbox code or contractor lockbox installed.

   c. The buyers' agent

      1. Keep weekly pressure on the agent to ensure that escrow is constantly moving forward and that time-frames are not being exceeded.

   d. The lender

      1. Ensure that the appraisal has been received back and at value.
      2. Get weekly updates to ensure that the buyers have furnished the lender with all required documentation and to stay ahead of any potential issues.

Some lenders and escrow officers might have 30 or more files on their desk at any one time, so a gentle reminder about your escrow should help move it back to the top of the stack. It is always astounding how often lenders blow by their scheduled close of escrow dates. This can lead to buyers losing the lock on their loan, and if rates have increased, it may disqualify the buyers from getting their loan. Stay in regular communication to keep the lender on track.

6. Respond appropriately to requests for repairs or lender required repairs. If your rehab has been effective, you have most likely dealt with the most pressing and expensive repair issues, but buyers and lenders often ask for any lingering health and safety issues to be addressed.

    a. If the buyers are asking for a huge credit or being unreasonable, push back hard and quickly since at this point you're better off getting these buyers out of the way and getting back on the market as quickly as possible.

    b. If you feel the request is acceptable, you agree to the repairs, and you've verified that the buyers' appraisal has been completed and the lender has all their necessary paperwork, proceed with the repairs in a timely fashion. The worst thing in the world is delaying your own escrow or holding up the escrow so long that the buyers lose their rate lock or worse yet, lose interest in your property. Timely repairs also show goodwill and will usually motivate everyone else to keep moving forward. If the repair request is more substantial, you'll have to evaluate it against your entire project and make a determination. Keep in mind that if it's a glaring problem, the next buyer will most likely ask for it to be fixed as well. Better to agree the first time, keep your first escrow going smoothly, and move on than to go back on the market, wait two more months, and sell for $10,000

less and still have to make the repair.
Once repairs are completed:

1. Forward all documentation to the buyers' agent.
2. Send any open invoices to the escrow officer to avoid delays later.

7. Don't forget your weekly visits to the property. Make sure that:

a. Weeds aren't growing, and the lawn is mowed with sharp edges.
b. Sprinklers are on in the summer.
c. Heat is on in the winter.
d. Newspapers aren't piled up on the doorstep.
e. There are no water leaks.
f. Low pool levels get filled.
g. The pool water is crystal clear.
h. The property is free of vagrants and trespassers.
i. There are no surprise repairs, damage, or vandalism.

You don't want the buyers to take their in-laws by to show off their soon-to-be dream home only to find dead grass, high weeds, and a dirty pool, especially if those in-laws might be helping them with the down payment.

Take pride in your project all the way to the close of escrow. This also protects you if you do have to go back on the market because you won't have to waste any time preparing should the need arise.

8. Continue to monitor:

a. The escrow officer
b. The lender
c. The buyer's agent
d. Your own agent if applicable

9. Review your estimated closing statement and ensure that:

   a. Payoff amounts are correct.
   b. You are getting the proper discount or binder credits if applicable.
   c. All open invoices are reflected.
   d. Commissions and other figures are accurate.

10. Schedule your signing once you have received the buyers' loan documents:

    a. Make sure you're available to sign. Remember that for some loans, the seller must sign before the buyers can sign. Let your escrow officer know if you're taking any vacations or extended absences. Again, you don't want to hold up your own escrow.

    b. During the signing, make a final review of all figures and credits.

11. Remove staging:

    a. Order stagers to remove the staging furniture.

       1. It might be wise to wait until the last minute just in case of a last-minute cancellation. Avoid going back on the market and having to re-stage a house.
       2. Communicate in advance with the stagers to make sure they'll be available on short notice during the final week of escrow.

    b. Confirm that staging is removed.

12. Upon closing, deliver all:

    a. Keys
    b. Garage door remotes
    c. Appliance warranties
    d. Any other pertinent information to the buyer

13. After closing, have the agent remove:

    a. Sign
    b. Flier box
    c. Lockbox

14. Transfer utilities:

    a. Make sure the buyers have received information to start all the property utility services in advance.
    b. Make sure you communicate your timelines and intentions with the buyers and their agent.

    If the buyers close on a Friday and haven't ordered services in their name, you could be paying their bills for up to a week if they're not diligent the following week. This is why we like to schedule closings on Wednesday or Thursdays.

    You also don't want your buyers' services getting cut off on their moving day. If these people have a great experience, you could be the person they call when they are looking for their next home.

15. *Pick up your check from the title company!*

CHAPTER 12

THE BACK-OFFICE

P eople who get up at 5:00 in the morning and go running didn't love doing that in the beginning. What they did first was make a decision to do it. They probably struggled the first 20 times, but they kept building, and pretty soon, they had a system and discipline, and then they fell in love with it. And now, it doesn't matter where they go; they are the ones who are getting out and doing some exercise or activity because they feel weird if they don't. They have learned to love the process.

Though it may sound impossible, we want you to learn to love your back-office process because of how great it will make you feel when it's working right. We wish we could tell you the back-office was sexy, but more often than not, it's pretty boring. However, the more boring your business can get, the more successful you can become. If you want not to be bored, jump out of a plane, go bungee jumping, or take a river rafting tour on a level-5 river. If you want to make the cash register ring, you want to be boring in the back-office. Your back-office is the backbone of your business. It doesn't matter how many houses you sell; if you don't have the right paperwork, you don't get paid. Always look at your back-office and all the paperwork in that back-office as money sitting on your desk.

Create a System

The back-office essentially is about a system. Your goal is to document your system so well that a sixth grader could come in and do it. McDonald's isn't the best restaurant in the world, but it is easily the most successful restaurant in the world. Why? It's because anyone can thrive there as an employee within the system they've created. You want to imitate that by creating a system that can work seamlessly with anyone who uses it. So once you have a system set up for your back-office, test it with an intern or your son, daughter, uncle, aunt, whoever it is, then look back and identify the gaps and fix them.

We no longer listen to our music on an 8-track, a cassette tape deck, or CDs. Please do not run your business like you're in 1985, with your bad mullet and your mesh ABBA T-shirt. Adapt to new technology and work like a professional and innovator.

In the beginning, you are going to make mistakes. "Anything worth doing well is worth doing poorly in the beginning." Thank you, Marshall Thurber. But we want you to get past that phase and into the phase of owning a business that someone could buy from you at some point in time.

The paperwork, disclosures, contracts with subcontractors and contractors, bookkeeping, and all of that can become overwhelming. We recommend "chunking" it down into manageable pieces. Even if it's just you at the beginning, this will allow you to have an easier time when your real estate investment business blows up. You may make one deal a year or 100 deals a year, either way it should be the same. Our goal for you is that you will do a 100 properties a year with ease and enjoy the life that you have always dreamed about. Your back-office system will help you achieve that.

Also, when you work with contractors, investors, your CPA or bookkeeper, and lenders, they will need information from you. You don't want to be looking through a shoebox full of papers when they need something; that can waste a lot of time. You want to know exactly where you can find this information so it never takes any of your time at all.

Jerry

For every home I have remodeled or built from scratch, I create a three-ring binder. It tells me what color the paint is for the various rooms, which tile or laminate flooring I used, who the contractors were with their contact information, and who the subcontractors were. That way, when I go into escrow, and I sit down with the buyers, I can pull up the binder and show them the work that has been done. Then they feel like they are dealing with a professional, and they don't feel like they are going into uncharted waters where they could get screwed—and we never want any of our customers to feel that way when they are buying one of our properties.

The Various Files

The good news is that this business is not super complicated. It's essentially compartmentalized into projects. For each property, as we have touched on in past chapters, you have your initial purchase paperwork and disclosures, which will be the *Acquisition File*. Once you own it and start generating expenses on it, you will have your QuickBooks or *Bookkeeping File* for the project. Depending on the level of engagement you have with the contractor, you may also have a separate *Rehab and Design File* where you keep plans, estimates, paint samples or photos for ideas, materials lists, and permit applications or paperwork. Finally, when you resell the property, you will have your *Resale File* for each project, which will include all the contracts, disclosures, and other transactional paperwork.

Some paperwork will overlap; for example, you will want to keep the initial acquisition closing statement in both your Acquisition File and in your Bookkeeping File. And the same on the backend; you will keep your *resale* closing statement in both the Resale File and the Bookkeeping File.

If your mind goes into panic mode when faced with a sea of paperwork, there is good news; there is help available. They are called Transaction Coordinators. Ask around or put an ad on Craigslist, and you will find several in your market. Even if you are good at paperwork but not experienced in real estate, this is a good first stop. Hire a Transaction Coordinator for one day for $20 per hour, and have them create a blank transaction file for you with every form, disclosure, sample report, communication log, marketing checklist, etc., so you can have a master file for that portion of your back-office. Since your

Acquisition File and your Resale File are mirror images of each other, now you already know what two-thirds of your back-office process will look like.

For your Bookkeeping File, do the same thing, but for this just ask your CPA or again put an ad on Craigslist searching for a bookkeeper, and you will get 10 applicants who will spend a day with you for $20 to $25 per hour. They can build your QuickBooks with a structure that works for flips, and if you met with them one day a month, that would be more than enough to keep all your bookkeeping up to speed.

Consider It a Revenue Driver, Not a Cost

Even though every project is different, every file is going to have the same things in it. And this brings up another point where you should start looking at your bookkeeping department not as a cost, but as a revenue driver. If you have clear bookkeeping from the very inception of a project, you can get a much clearer picture of each project. For example, even as the project is getting ready to close escrow, you will be able to project ahead and see that you will have one more PG&E bill and that the bill for the last-minute escrow repairs hasn't been invoiced yet. If you can stay on top of these things in real time, you will be able to accurately divide profits at the close of escrow when working with partners.

Terence

Before my bookkeeping was running smoothly, I would close my partner escrows and divide the profits, and then five more bills would show up! Suddenly, I was paying another $850 in last minute bills.

The solution here is to hold back a little out of each project for these kinds of issues and then do a final accounting 30 days later, or be more predictive in your bookkeeping and project ahead for the last utility bills, property tax refunds, or last minute repairs. It's time-consuming and unprofessional to chase after your partners two weeks after a closing and ask for $425 back, so try to do it right on the front end. It's also one more item on your list that slows you down from finding that next property. This is the same thing the escrow company does. They estimate a few of the final bills higher and then usually send you a small refund check after the final accounting is done.

With proper bookkeeping, you will also know where you are in a project at every stage of the process. So if you are in escrow on the resale, and the buyers ask for a $500 repair, you can assess that against your bottom line, which can help you make those decisions. You might see that you are making $40,000, so it makes sense to give up the $500 and get this one closed, or you might see that you have already given away the farm, you aren't making much, and you might be better off pushing back hard. Or you are about to go negative and just need to get out of this property and on to the next one. It will at least give you clarity.

Hire Others

The back-office is all about leverage. There is a great book called *The 4-Hour Work Week* that tells how you can leverage your time. Make sure that someone else is doing the monotony, dotting the i's and crossing the t's. Get a scanner if you don't have one. Your phone probably has an app that can scan. If it doesn't, a scanner costs less than $40. Then if you are at the point where you want to get an assistant, you can seek help at a great website called Upwork.com.

Jerry

I love Upwork.com and other sites like it. I have a virtual personal assistant who I pay $350 a month, and this person takes care of my emails and my calendar, so when I wake up, my day is set for me. They are coming out with new software all the time to make life more efficient so you can get more done. Use those tools. Remember, the goal isn't to save time through leverage so you can clean your desk or wash your car. It is so you can have the 30,000-foot view of the business. This will enable you to do the things in the business that bring in the most revenue and that will springboard your business.

If you can create a good system and have someone else do the monotonous tasks, you can spend your time aquiring projects and finding the people with money to finance them. The goal is to make a system that will allow you to live your *why*.

It's important to find out what you need from the people you want to hire. If you are just starting up, you don't need to hire somebody who wants to be out in the field writing offers because your business isn't there yet. What you want to do is hire someone who has the skills that you lack. The chain is only as strong as the weakest link, so find somebody who is super strong in the areas you aren't.

Jerry

I headhunted someone who loves paperwork, filing, and having everything in its place. She loves it when I say, "Hey, do you know where that document is?" By the time I finish the sentence, she has pulled out the document.

She was at a very successful law firm in Los Angeles, but I knew she didn't love living there. I offered her less money than she was making, but in a more desirable place, closer to her family.

Now she has been with me making my life easy for over a decade. One time while I was traveling the world, I was doing five real estate projects, and all of them were being handled with ease. And now, even though I live in Costa Rica, my business is handled for me in the States. I get the emails and the things that are important for me to handle, but the other things are handled brilliantly by my assistant extraordinaire.

Terence

We all have specific areas of our businesses or lives that we love and other areas that we don't love so much. I love looking for deals; I love the excitement of real estate auctions, the thrill of winning an auction or getting a low offer accepted; and I love the process of design and construction. My weakness is paperwork and follow-up. What makes it even worse for me is that I know this business so well that I know exactly what should be done at every single step of the process. But if it comes down to writing disclosures or going to look at a new fixer that just came on the market, I have always tended to procrastinate on my paperwork and go look at houses.

It goes back to building your team. It took me years to figure out, but I finally added the right people to fill in the gaps in my system. You may enjoy paperwork and bookkeeping, but perhaps your head swims after looking at two houses, or you never know how to communicate with contractors. If that is the case, maybe you will run the back-office yourself. I am not a back-office person, but I still had to build my back-office system for someone else to run.

Use a Personality Test

If you find people you think are awesome, and you want to bring them into your business, have them take a personality test. There are several different options, but the best would be Myers-Briggs Type Indicator (MBTI), the Kolbe A Index, and the DiSC. Myers-Briggs has an on-line test that can be taken for a fee. You can learn about any of these on Wikipedia and see which one sounds like the best fit for you. They are worth doing because they will show you right away who your candidates are and if they are suited for the positions. The results of the test will also show you how they might interact with you, which is also important. The tests are amazingly accurate and could save you thousands and thousands of dollars in retraining and rehiring. Don't have them take the test after you hire them—do it before.

Jerry

I have a friend who owns a massive CPA firm with over 100 employees, and at that firm they go through three different interviews with people and have them take a Kolbe test. If the Kolbe test doesn't turn out the way that they like, they won't hire the interviewees no matter how good they think they are. They feel it's that accurate and that important.

So build the system, and if you don't have the skills or desire to run your back-office, use other people's skills to not just grow your business but, more importantly, keep your business from stalling. If you hate paperwork, it will also take all that negativity off your plate and allow you to do the $300-per-hour work that you were born to do.

CHAPTER 13

REPEAT 100 TIMES/ THE SYSTEM

N
ow you might be up for finding one of these projects, but the thought of doing 100 projects seems unthinkable, undoable, unfathomable. Yes, it may take some time, and it definitely won't happen overnight, but if you implement the system, it will begin to happen somewhat automatically.

If you find that you are spending the bulk of your time on Home Depot runs, wiping down countertops, and putting keys in lockboxes or signs in the ground, you might want to reevaluate your system. Think about investing in a Fortune 500 Company. Would you invest in the company if the CEO was spending his time on the assembly line, or sweeping the floors of the factory? Yes, when that Fortune 500 Company was in its infancy, its founder may or may not have been doing some of those tasks, so in the very beginning of your business, you may be doing every function—and you should since it will give you an understanding of how long these tasks take and what kind of employee you might need to complete them. But in the long term, you should be at the very top of the pyramid, right on that sharp point, directing everything below you, finding opportunities, finding money, and feeding that into your assembly line. This is the Fortune 500 work. If you can get to this point, if you can run your business like a CEO, you will find yourself making CEO money.

On your first flip, you might agonize for days over picking tile for a shower, but after you have done a few projects and you know what works, this is a five-minute decision at The Home Depot or looking at a few samples with your contractors. Your first flip might take you dozens of phone calls to figure out pricing for paint, flooring, roofing, drywall, HVAC, windows, and electrical. But again, after you have encountered every problem a house can have, you will know these numbers better than your contractors.

> ## Terence
> I meet with subcontractors and other vendors all the time and just by going through the scale of the project and the amount of material needed, I can come up with a pretty good guess for what their bid is going to be. Sometimes they go away for two to three days, sometimes 10 days before coming back to me with their carefully calculated estimate and lo and behold, it's within $100 of the number I crunched out on the back of an envelope in three minutes.

Earlier, we talked about true mastery, which comes after 10,000 hours of dedication. You won't master this process on the first project, but if you follow our system and better yet, get a little bit of coaching, you can start out with a winner, and over time you will reach your own level of mastery. We hope we can save you at least the first 9,000 hours by sharing everything we have learned in our nearly 40 years of combined real estate experience. If you are interested in jumpstarting your investment career, contact us through our website www.flippingmainstreet.com. We would be happy to set up a coaching plan for you that's a perfect match for your personality, team, and market.

Think About the Big Picture

It isn't just the time spent that matters, however. There also must be the dedication and the true desire to learn. If you're not interested in design, construction, housing, investing, people, or money, then you somehow wandered into the wrong aisle of Barnes & Noble.

Say that you're just in it for the money. Then why not at least try to think a little broader and consider the jobs you're creating and directing to people you know and care about. Think about the relationships and often the friendships this close contact and camaraderie can foster. Or think about the higher quality of housing you can provide for families in your community. For you to have a million-dollar business—to generate $1 million in the economy of your town—it doesn't take that many projects. It might only be eight or 10 deals. Don't just think about the $100,000 you made from the 10 mediocre deals. Think of the fact that you generated over $1 million into the local economy because of your business. Keep that mindset of adding value, and you will create an ecosystem of success and a lot of fans of your business.

The raving fans we want in this business are our private lenders, partners, contractors, subcontractors, escrow people, inspectors, home warranty sales people, cleaners, stagers, Realtors, mortgage brokers, and buyers. When you have those fans, you will hit that 100-mark so fast that you will be shocked. You will look back at not only the money it generated for you and your family and the time and freedom it gave you but also what it gave to all the people you were in contact with, which is hundreds of people in the long term.

If you do everything right, you can operate with total transparency. What most investors don't realize is that even if the buyers of your properties have their own agents, those buyers are ultimately your customers. If you have bought the property right, you can afford to make them happy. Unlike most self-professed gurus who constantly seem to be trying to pull one over on their poor unsuspecting dupe buyers, we believe that to build a lasting business, you should be striving for happy customers. You don't hear Nike, Honda, Apple, or any other successful business talking about trying to take advantage of their customers like that. Your customers should be lifelong fans of your brand.

Terence

This is not a charity project, but if it comes down to saving $100 or picking an excellent feature for a home—giving someone granite countertops instead of Formica, an awesome master bathroom, or a clean, functional tub that they can bathe kids in, I admit I always err on the side of providing a quality product.

Some of our colleagues and competitors would argue against this, and some of them may have netted more on each project than we have, but we think that to last in this business, you must have more than one dimension to your daily work and process. If all you care about is making that extra $100, it's a pretty hollow victory when you get it. Don't try to squeeze every ounce of juice out of each negotiation. When you make $40,000 on a flip and provided someone with the nicest home they are ever going to live in, and all the subcontractors made a decent wage, and your escrow people got the business, and your hard money lender made $8,000 in interest, now that is what we consider a true victory. When every one of your projects becomes a win-win-win-win-win, you have reached the level of mastery we wish for you.

When every one of your projects generates this much positive energy and momentum, you become unstoppable and getting on to the next project becomes exciting and not a chore, work, a challenge, or stress.

Terence

The other night, I was in my home office working late on a spreadsheet. I have eight projects going, a book in the making, three amazing kids I spend every available moment with, and several other projects underway. You might think I was stressed out. Honestly I'm not feeling stressed in the slightest. I'm busier than I have ever been but having more fun in my business than I have ever had.

Keep Yourself Accountable

As you are building your repeatable system, it pays to start with yourself. You didn't like working for a boss or supervisor who was too strict, but you had better make sure that you are not too easy a boss, especially to yourself.

Jerry

I haven't had an actual physical job for nearly 17 years. All I have done is invest, and I wouldn't trade it for anything. I have traveled the world and seen most of the 100 things most travel books recommend seeing. It's an amazing feeling to be able to do that, and it is something we all can do.

When I evaluate my productivity, I don't judge my days because I have had days when I have been sick or feeling poorly. Instead, I judge my weeks. How did I do this week? Did I accomplish what I wanted to this week?

I'm the CEO of me, and I have an imaginary board of directors. At the end of the week, I ask my imaginary board of directors (I know this sounds silly, but I do it), would I get fired this week based on what I have done? There have been plenty of weeks when I have canned myself. The next week, I have had to hire a better me to do the job.

Terence

The imaginary board of directors is a great metaphor for evaluating yourself: deciding each week if you should be fired or not or maybe even given a bonus or promotion. Then if you get fired, you must rehire a better "you" each week. What if, after a week where you were fired, you had to put together a new resume and interview for your job all over again? What new skills, plans, and strategies would you bring to the table to convince the board to hire you back?

> If you're not bringing a new plan and a new desire and motivation, you are better off staying on unemployment. If you are getting fired every week, you need to dig deep and make some big changes in yourself and your plan.

Many people flounder with no supervision, oversight, or prodding, so if you aren't good at self-starting and staying motivated, make sure you build a system that will allow someone other than yourself to monitor your production and keep you from procrastinating or getting distracted. Find a coach, a mentor, a friend, a colleague—anyone you can communicate comfortably with who will take five minutes each week to review your Task List and check in with you a few times to make sure you're checking things off your list.

Ideally, you do this every day because when you are working for yourself or are between projects, it's easy to burn days. When you realize that with a proper focus, every day could offer the chance to find another great opportunity, you understand that it's far too expensive to lose that time.

Terence

A quick thought on coaching: My kids won't listen to me, yet they have perfect behavior at school, they listen to other parents, their teachers, coaches, piano teachers, etc. Even as adults we do the same; we know exactly what we should do, but we don't listen to ourselves or sometimes to the ones closest to us. If your spouse tells you to call someone back, you almost refuse to do it out of principle. But if a coach told you, you would do it. Quit getting in your own way and sign up for one of our Accountability Programs today at www.flippingmainstreet.com. Even though you already know what to do, let us help you listen to yourself!

> ## Jerry
> We wrote this book as an homage to the success we have had. I love the quote, "If I have seen further, it is by standing on the shoulders of giants." (Sir Isaac Newton). Choose the right giants and make sure they are pointing you in the right direction.

Don't work in a vacuum; opportunities come from getting out and coming in contact with the greatest number of people, situations, conversations, and opportunities. Fuel with more surface area burns more easily. Kindling has a lot of nooks and crannies and surfaces relative to its mass, but a big heavy log has less surface area for its mass and is harder to light.

Also, you must have the money, back-office systems, organization and management systems, and procedures to keep the fire burning. In your day to day, we want you to be burning fast and bright! We don't want you spending nine months working on one project with one lender and only one chance of success; we want you burning hot and fast with five projects going and five more in escrow and lenders and contractors lining up to do business with you!

Sometimes you lose focus, but the key is to continue the process. You can jump back in at any time. Just get back out there and shine, get bright and hot, talk to people and make the opportunities happen. As long as you're still smoldering just a little bit, you can always throw a little kindling and a couple of logs back on, and you're blazing. It won't take long before the campers must step back from that fire! As long as you have the desire, no one can kill your business. Even after a colossal failure, you can put yourself right back into a winning project, a new winning partnership. Never stop smoldering; never give up.

Achieve Wealth

Picture the yachts, the girls in bikinis, the expensive cars, the bling, and the pool parties—now get back to work and reality. The wealthiest real estate investors are typically the guys and girls in jeans they bought at T.J. Maxx, driving five-plus-year-old cars with no payment, and living in houses well below their means, so they have more money for their investing.

If your foundation is strong, you can outlast any bad project, bad market, or bad news. If you are spending money faster than you're making it and getting behind on your taxes and savings, you have your priorities wrong. If you are always spending below your earnings, your wealth is always growing. If you can teach just one of your children the same business and same principles, that becomes a legacy. It is very rare but very possible. Most wealth disappears after one generation. Think what it could become for your great grandchildren if you create a clear path for them to follow.

One of the greatest *whys* of this business is that it is a fun, creative and liberating way to earn a living. So as one of our investor friends said, "When my wife wants to blow some money shopping, I give her $3,000 and send her to The Home Depot to buy things for our next flip." That may not fulfill every woman's shopping fantasy, but you get the idea. If you make the business rewarding and positive, you won't constantly be looking for escapes and distractions.

The business is also not very fun or productive when you are juggling bills, stalling off vendors, and getting charged hundreds of dollars a month in late fees. That quickly becomes the biggest stress in your life, and the biggest time waster of the business. It puts you on a downward cycle of missing opportunities, alienating your best workers, and losing sleep and quality time with your family and friends. Stay positive, stay focused, and stay way ahead of your bills for constant and lasting growth and the chance to leave a legacy.

Why do this 100 times? It is easy math. If you want to make $1 million, then you only have to make $10,000 on each property, and you're there. If you are a first-time investor starting out, you are probably not going to do 100 projects in your first year. You might do four or five, or you might do 10. If you do 10 projects a year for the next 10 years, you will go through at least one cycle where you might make $10,000 on some and $100,000 on others. It's going to go up and down. If you do it right and follow the system, chances are you won't make $1 million in 10 years—you'll make multiple millions. It all depends on your desire and your system.

Jerry

Someone once said, "No one ever learned something they didn't want to." You might say, "Wait, I learned multiplication tables." Yes, and I also learned every country in Africa when I was taking geography, but I probably couldn't rattle off more than five of those countries to you now. I memorized them for a short time, and then I went to what was important to me and what I wanted to learn.

At first, you may not even know what you love. You want to have more time, more freedom, and more money, and then along the path, the thing you are really interested in will suddenly pop out.

Terence loves analyzing projects. I love architecture and looking at real estate. When I walk into a house, I can feel if it's a winner. It comes from experience and opening myself up to be great at it.

You become either an example or a warning to your children, friends, and family. So be an example and inspire others to live a life of creativity and fulfillment. Use the system because it will give you the 30,000-foot view of your goals, your life, and your future.

Go out there and start property number 1 of 100.

CHAPTER 14

RELAX, RETIRE, OR RELINQUISH

If you do everything right, this chapter sums up the crossroads where we expect you to find yourself. Depending on the scale of the system you build, this could be in as little as three to five years, or it could be in 10 to 20 years. We hope that you have not only flipped 100 or more homes, but that by keeping your spending in check, you have been able to keep 15 to 20 homes as rentals, and that you have accumulated so much cash that you are able to use low-interest credit lines and a lot of your own funds to finance your projects.

So what to do now? You have lots of options; the world is yours at this point. If you are like us, and you love every nuance of this crazy business, then keep going. Slow down a little, or keep growing; it's all about you and your goals. If you would still rather walk through a newly acquired house that smells like bad tenants than take a tour down the Rhine, then just keep doing what you love.

Relax

If you and your spouse do want to start touring the world, or you want to start working on that novel you have always dreamed of writing, then just slow down a little. You don't have to have 10 projects going, but you can keep one or two real estate plates spinning without too much effort. You have built the system, so why not use it?

Retire

If you have lost your love of the business, or you are feeling burned out, sure, you can retire, keep collecting some rent or interest checks, and find hobbies you enjoy or spend more time with family and friends.

But if you've built your system correctly, you've most likely been doing this along the way.

Relinquish

One of the hardest, but maybe most rewarding options is to relinquish. Perhaps you find yourself with three grown children with two college degrees each. None has found his or her niche in life, and they are all living at least three states away. Why not use your business as the ultimate bait to lure them home? Offer them jobs in your flip business with the possibility of an equity partnership once they prove themselves. You can't offer this right out of the gate, or they won't appreciate what you are offering. They have to perceive the value.

Teach them the business. If they are like our kids, they have probably been around it forever, so they should remember enough at least to pick it up quickly. You can also match the positions to their strengths. If one of your children just likes manual labor and a simple life, he can be your painter, tile-setter, trash-out guy, or gopher at $18 per hour. He will probably pad the timecard a little and take long lunches, and he might talk back, but you were going to let the business go anyway, remember? Maybe your daughter loves design and numbers. If so, put her in charge of the books and project planning. If you have a son who loves finding opportunities, help him get his real estate license and make him your property hunter. The opportunities are endless, and you get to spend every day with the ones you love.

Will they frustrate you? Will there be drama with them or their spouses? Maybe, but you are giving yourself the chance of creating a legacy. Instead of your kids inheriting your 20 houses and a business they know nothing about and dumping them for 80 cents on the dollar or less if they live out of the area, now they are going to continue to build on everything you have done. They don't need the cash, and if they keep the system going, they will be doing the same thing with your grandchildren 30 years from now. That is a compelling reason to go to work every day and build this system. Your great grandchildren might be taking over a 500-house empire with a contracting business, real estate brokerage, mortgage brokerage, and more. The system is completely elastic; it can stretch to fit whatever size business you can dream up.

If you do relinquish to your children, you will have to get out of the way and let them fail a little and hopefully succeed a lot. That is how you learned, so why are you trying to teach them with only a curriculum of success?

Maybe you don't have kids, or you hate yours. That's okay too. We hope that by helping you build a solid, repeatable business with clear books and records of past performance, you have something that someone else will be willing to buy. If it's a multi-faceted business with lots of strong components and a great track record, it might be worth a small fortune in itself. So if you're done and want a clean break, don't just let it dwindle or die; sell it at its peak and reap the benefits of your creativity and persistence. Notice we didn't say hard work, though there is probably going to be some of that too.

Jerry

Terence and I knew a property manager who was bringing in over $10,000 a month, and when he decided to retire, he didn't ask anybody if they wanted the business; he just closed the doors. I happened to be one of his clients with a whole lot of properties, and I had to find another property manager. Had his business included clear, repeatable systems, he certainly could have sold it or brought in a partner or employee to continue operating it. Keep this in mind as you're developing your business, and you will create multiple options for lasting income or a successful retirement.

Whatever your exit plan is, our most sincere wish is that the business we have helped you to create has given you a lifetime of fulfillment, growth, happiness, and financial reward.

Some Final Thoughts on the "Business" of Flipping Houses

Terence

If you own a restaurant, a hair salon, or even a real estate sale business, you are heavily affected by competition, by the economy, and most of all by fickle customers. I have lost dozens of escrows throughout my career over buyers changing their minds and sellers refusing to make needed repairs or accept reasonable prices for their properties. I have also lost opportunities to competing agents who were sometimes much less experienced and qualified than me. Flipping houses became more and more attractive to me as I realized that I could ultimately be in control of my own business and destiny.

Of course, there is still potential for competition. I just closed escrow on a bank-owned house that came on the market at $51,500. There were 21 offers on the house, and I was the winning bidder at $84,100. It was still a great deal, by the way.

The difference is that of the 21 bidders, 15 were unrealistically trying to get the house for $60,000 or less. Because they didn't understand the costs or hadn't had time to get detailed estimates, they felt like they had to pad the purchase price. These were local business people who were willing to flip the house if they could make $50,000 or more. They would have had to pay Realtor fees, rely on more expensive contractors, and take time away from their regular businesses to focus on the renovation project.

For me, this house was just more raw material for my system that is already churning away. Because I am doing this all the time, I know my costs up front. I already know what I'm going to do to the house and how much it will sell for when I'm done. My management system is in place, my renovation system is in place and ready for more work, and my sales and marketing systems is in place.

I know that on a bad day, my purchase at $84,100 should net me $20,000 in less than 120 days, and that in a perfect world, I might make $30,000 in 75 to 90 days.

In reality, I'm only competing with five or six other people in my market. If my system is leaner and faster and since I'm doing more projects, I can afford to make a little less on each, and I can afford to spend an extra $3,000 or $4,000 on each project because I make it up on the back-end. I will do this on a "finish-only" project, meaning that the house just needs paint, flooring, countertops, fixtures, and maybe windows. This one was built in the 1980s and is conventional construction with a good roof and recent HVAC, so it is a four-week rehab without too many mysteries. These are the types of projects on which you can give up a little profit to add to your assembly line. Had this been a 1950s house with lots of unknowns, I would have been one of those bidders in the $60,000s or probably wouldn't have bought it at all.

In this case, even though I was competing against 21 people in my market, it's better than most industries. As the market has improved over the last few years, our local Board of Realtors membership has jumped from around 500 back up to over 800. At the height of the market in 2006, it was nearly 1,200. So even as there were more opportunities and higher prices, the pot was being divided among many more participants. While a good market may bring out a few more flippers, it is still very difficult for most people to come up with cash or find a way to borrow hundreds of thousands of dollars to flip a home without a proven system. A hot market with higher prices keeps a lot of competition away, yet a down market with low prices is a hard time to find cash to borrow. When I was trying to grow my real estate brokerage, several of my agents who I had trained and spent money to develop left to become brokers themselves. I always told my surgeon and attorney friends that they were lucky their assistants couldn't become competitors by taking a $200 class and passing a test with a score of 70% or better.

The other good news about competition in flipping is that it can breed opportunity as well. As an agent or surgeon or attorney or hairdresser, I want as few competitors as possible, but sometimes in flipping, a competitor can make you a lot of money. When I was regularly working the courthouse steps for trustee sales, I couldn't help but become friends with most of my "rivals." After all, we had a lot to talk about and a lot in common. In the last five years, I have partnered or collaborated with six of my former rivals on various flips. There are five others I will probably end up working with on future projects.

Turn Rivals into Partners

If you can constantly turn rivals into partners, your success will grow exponentially. Imagine you are a quarterback facing a brutal defense, and you're getting sacked every play. Suddenly, you realize you can start converting the other team's defensive linebackers into your own offensive line or receivers. How much easier does it become to score touchdowns? Pretty soon there is no one left to stop you, and you're just walking it into the end zone every play. You can do the same thing in your flip business.

Even if you are not doing projects together, these once rivals can be a great sounding board for projects. Sometimes you stare at a property so long that it's hard to remain unbiased. That is when it helps to have an outside, but expert perspective. If you can build these friendships, you never know when they may call you and tell you about a property they saw that they couldn't buy, but they will spin to you for a percentage or simply for a future lunch or favor in return.

The Job Security of Flipping Houses

While markets change (and you have to be aware of the cycles), what doesn't change are people. Sadly, there will always be deaths, divorces, drug addiction, job losses, ignorance, bad tenants, conflict, apathy, bad luck, leaking faucets, fires, and more. So if you ever think that there won't be another junky house to buy and fix up, dream on; the cycle is endless.

> ## Terence
> I have driven by many of the houses I have sold, sometimes only a few months or weeks later, and found them with lawns overgrown, junky cars in the driveway, and towels or blankets hung in the windows with five dogs barking inside. These are houses that I put blood, sweat, tears, and granite into, and just weeks later they are back to looking like fixers.

The majority of people don't understand what it takes to maintain a home, even on a basic level. Most of them should remain tenants and let someone else take care of them, but they watch too many HGTV shows, and they think they can do it. Once they have kids, work, stress, and a myriad of other responsibilities and costs, the house becomes the last priority. And that is where you come in, ready to take advantage of these endless opportunities. We hope that by doing so, you will enrich yourself, your family and friends, and even your community.

Don't Let the Barriers Stop You
With flipping, while there are some barriers to entry, like not having access to capital or the right knowledge, the greatest barrier is the mental barrier that people impose on themselves. If there is anything we accomplish with this book, we hope it will be removing whatever mental barriers you are putting on yourself. There are thousands of agents, contractors, and other entrepreneurs who have all the ability in the world to enter this business and thrive yet remain in a position of doing the work for someone else.

Terence

I know at least 30 agents and contractors just in my market who have all the connections, knowledge, and ability to flip houses successfully, but the thought of doing it is overwhelming to them. They think there is too much risk or too many headaches, yet they are doing equally stressful escrows or projects for other people to make $2,000 to $6,000 in commissions or profits when with almost the same effort they could be making $15,000 to $30,000 or more. Not only that, but they could also be making the decisions that affect their livelihood rather than waiting for clients to make a decision or dealing with clients who always make wrong decisions that cost them a commission or fee. Or worse yet, they are dealing with clients who constantly get mad or emotional when they face any challenges or bad news during their escrow or project.

We hate to see people miss opportunities, or even a real calling, simply out of fear. We have done it all and seen it all, and lived to tell. We have been to the edge of the real estate world, and we are back to tell you that those giant sea serpents on the map are only drawn there because the mapmaker had a wild imagination. It is safe; you can do this. You do have to learn the business, you do have to work a system, and you do have to develop some mental toughness and discipline. But trust us, this is easier to do than most of the jobs other people have to do.

What price do you put on your freedom, both emotional and financial? They are both priceless. So for the cost of this book, or the cost of a little coaching, or the cost in time to learn how to build your business the right way, isn't it worth it?

Terence

Today I stayed home with my sick 12-year-old son and borrowed the grandparents for an hour to sneak out to see my 15-year-old son's school performance. And tomorrow I'm taking my 17-year-old daughter to the orthodontist. Are any of these activities slowing down my eight projects? No, because my system operates without me. It's not a perpetual motion machine. I do have to put some energy into it occasionally, but it can operate without me for a few days out of every week.

Did you get that? Try telling your boss at the bank or the post office or the doctor's office where you work that you are going to start missing a few days each week and that you want a 300% raise. Let us know how that goes. If it works, maybe we will buy your book. If it doesn't work, then you have done the right thing by buying ours.

Jerry

Since you have built a great system, your business is going to be flexible. Sometimes there will be fewer opportunities, but if you set up a system, and you can leverage your resources—for example, a landscaping portion of your business—when there are not a lot of projects, you will still be able to make money. If there are too many projects, then you can leverage the contracting part of your business. There are always ways to bring in money.

I firmly believe that there are always more than enough opportunities. I never go into the luck process. Right now I am living in Costa Rica. The average price for homes in Nosara, is on the low end of $350,000. I just bought a condo for $92,000, and all I need to do with it is update the kitchen, a cost of $4,500, and put it back on at $150,000 next season. There are always more than enough opportunities. If it doesn't sell, it rents at over $1,200 a month. Not bad, huh?

You only have one life, so do something you love and enjoy, something that stretches you and allows you to be creative. If you don't, all of a sudden, years have passed, and you will think, "I should have gone on that trip; I should have spent more time with my kids; I should have written the book; I should have opened up that business." Don't should all over yourself. Get out there and take a little action. It will be worth it a thousand-fold.

We do this so that we can grow and give. We have gotten to a point where we have the luxury of teaching others what we have learned over the last 20 years. We are living the dream. We love what we do—we love real estate. If it all started over again, guess what we would be doing? Real estate. Take all the knowledge you now possess and get to work, if that's what you even want to call this fantastic new lifestyle that you are about to enjoy. Start living a life worth documenting. And remember, we are here to help.

Now What?

It's 11 o'clock at night, you have just finished reading the book, and you're feeling excited about the potential of doubling or tripling your income, not having to go to work, and having more time for building a life. But how do you get there from here?

There is always variation. The Universe has never found a straight line. Some days are going to be better than other because of this. Each one, however, is getting you closer to being financially successful. You can start small, but you do have to start. Like going into a pool, the first step feels cold; then it's okay for a while. Once you get in up to your waist, it's rough; then you force yourself to dive in. This will be the same, so just stick your toe in by going back to Chapters 1, 2, and 3. You don't even have to go back; we will paraphrase them for you right now. Or if you're ready, just get yourself psyched up and dive in. Just be smart about it, so you don't hit your head on the bottom.

Chapter 1, The Why. Why are you doing this? Go look at your kids sleeping and think about loading up their college funds and securing their future or having the freedom to take them on a great vacation before they are out of the house and that opportunity is lost forever. If your goal is to get out of a financial hole, envision the bills coming in. Oh wait! There are no bills because they are all on auto-pay now, and your accounts have plenty of money to pay everything. How would that feel? What could you do with the time and energy you spend just worrying about money? So get a good grasp on your *why* again right now.

Chapter 2, Become a Student. Go to a trustee sale or take someone, anyone involved in the business of flipping houses to lunch or coffee tomorrow! Call three agents! Spend two hours browsing inventory on Zillow or agents' websites.

Chapter 3, The Plan. Get a yellow tablet, go to Starbucks tomorrow, and start mapping out your plan. Make a list of everyone you know, especially in real estate, banking, construction, design, accounting, cleaning, staging, or anyone who can push a broom or lawnmower. Build the best team you can. Look back at Chapter 3 and make it happen.

We have done everything we can for now; now you must do something. Anything. It's actually going to be easy. We don't want you to be the person who 20 years from now says, "Oh, yeah, I took a real estate course or read a real estate book once," or "I invested once, and it didn't work." We want you to experience exponential growth. We don't want to give you one fish; we want to teach you how to fish. Or even teach you how to build a fishing fleet.

We've proven that the opportunity is real, abundant, and repeatable. Now, the only thing missing is you! You have everything you need and more. So get out there and push yourself to do something bigger, something bolder than anything you've done in the past. You'll be amazed at what you can accomplish by simply taking the first step.

Good luck and happy flipping.

Jerry & Terence

ABOUT THE AUTHORS

Terence's Bio

Terence and I have been going to the same school since 1979, so you might say I am an expert on Terence Davis, and I would agree with that statement.

I could share Terence's long list of accomplishments, and who knows, this might warrant being further down the list, but I wanted to start with who Terence is as a person. He is kind, patient, funny, and incredibly loyal. He is one of the most creative people I have ever spent time with, and he drops industry-changing ideas, no matter the industry, weekly. Terence is an incredible father. I think this is one of the strongest attributes of his character. He is there for his children on all counts—games, rehearsals, performances, doctor appointments, and putting them to bed at night. He is an incredibly supportive and available friend. These are all things he is able to do while running and growing an incredibly successful business.

Terence could have been anything. After graduating from UCLA (I know, I know, but it was the only school that would take him), he worked in the entertainment industry on multiple levels. He has written two children's books, he is an amazing coach, and he could sell anything. He loves real estate, but his passion, whether he can admit it or not, is helping people. I have seen him direct clients out of properties that would have made him tons of money. He has people's best interest in mind when he takes them on as clients, and you just don't see that a lot in the real estate business. The reason for this is that Terence is very empathetic. I think this is what makes him so great at our business and life. He can understand what people are going through, and his main focus is what is best for them.

It has been my privilege and pleasure to call him a partner, and more importantly, a friend for over 40 years. I'm not sure how many people know, but Terence was responsible for getting me into real estate investing, and I will never forgive him for it.

I have had more fun with Terence in the last 20 years of us working together than people who are supposed to be working should have. We sometimes laugh so hard that it leads to tears. I think his perspective is so wide and deep because he understands that whenever we begin something new, he can come from a place of deep curiosity, focus, and intensity, and also have the joy, silliness, and humor, and that is the magic of working with Terence Davis.

He, of course, is an idiot.

Jerry Agee

Jerry's Bio

Jerry Agee was born in Las Vegas on Valentine's Day in the early 1970s. Everything you would naturally assume based on these three facts is correct: He is tacky, over-the-top, and sickeningly romantic, but also compelling, lots of fun, and capable of creating vast fortunes.

Other intriguing facts about Jerry are that he could and did grow a full beard by the end of sixth grade, once caused an elementary school lockdown after being called out during a softball game (he really was safe), and played a fierce lead guitar for a rock band called V.A.T. (Vicious Animalistic Thing).

With little more than $1,000, a credit card, and a tube of ChapStick, he built a multi-million dollar real estate portfolio in just a few years while still traveling and snowboarding more than anyone I've ever known.

Unlike many entrepreneurs who closely guard their secrets, Jerry has constantly inspired and generously shared his strategies for investing in real estate with friends, family, colleagues, and strangers, much to their benefit.

A phenomenal friend and father, he's gone to great lengths to raise children who I believe will be amazing people filled with curiosity, passion for life, and deep empathy for others.

Terence Davis

Made in the USA
Las Vegas, NV
16 November 2023